Blow a Bubble
Not a Gasket

101 Ways to Reduce Stress and Add FUN to Your Life

Blow a Bubble Not a Gasket

101 Ways to Reduce Stress and Add FUN to Your Life

Janie Walters

QUAIL RIDGE PRESS
Brandon, Mississippi

Library of Congress Cataloging-in-Publication Data

Walters, Janie, 1948-
    Blow a bubble not a gasket : 101 ways to reduce stress and
    add fun to your life / Janie Walters.
        p. cm.
    Includes bibliographical references.
    ISBN 1-893062-39-2
        1. Conduct of life. 2. Stress management. I. Title.

BF637.C5 W34 2002
6158.1—dc21   2002029166

9 8 7 6 5 4 3

ISBN-10: 1-893062-39-2 • ISBN-13: 978-1-893062-39-9

Design by Cynthia Clark.
Printed in the United States of America.

QUAIL RIDGE PRESS
P. O. Box 123 • Brandon, MS 39043 • 1-800-343-1583
email: info@quailridge.com • www.quailridge.com

Dedication

My husband's name is Dickie. His name is really Dickie, not Richard. Dickie Harrison Walters. Our wedding invitation said, "Come have fun with Dick and Jane." For more than two decades now, we have been "having fun." During at least eight of those years, Dickie has had special fun hauling me from one writing retreat to another writing retreat, encouraging me to finish this book. I'm a starter. He's a finisher. *Blow a Bubble Not a Gasket* would have never existed if Dickie had not kept me focused on the goal. I not only love Dickie Walters, but I am eternally grateful to him for helping make my dream a reality. Thank you, Dickie. This book is dedicated to you.

Table of Contents

Section II Social Fun 73

Section III Mental Fun 113

SECTION IV Emotional Fun 155

Section V Spiritual Fun 203

Acknowledgments 227

Bibliography 229

Introduction

When our stress level is high, the last thing we need to do is read a 419-page manual titled "Governmental Theories On Stress Reduction." Let's face it, by the time most of us realize we are stressed, many symptoms have already appeared: high blood pressure, sleepless nights, migraine headaches, all compounded by the fact that we are gritting our teeth, breaking pencils, hollering at the children, kicking the dog, and honking viciously at highway offenders.

Unlike a laborious manual, *Blow a Bubble Not a Gasket* is designed to pull the plug on stress, offering 101 easy-to-read suggestions for reducing stress and replacing it with fun!

Time has always been scarce, but in the 21st century, it has become a precious commodity. Both children and adults are booked solid from early morning to late at night. Relax! This handy little book was written with that issue in mind. Here are 101 short, lighthearted suggestions that can each be read in a moment's time. No need to read them all at once unless you want to. Each idea is a complete entity.

Time is not the only stress producer. Tragedies, sicknesses, deadlines, broken relationships, finances, fear, angry words—all these and more—are capable of knocking our spirits, souls, and bodies to the ground. This book will not prevent that from happening. But, how long we stay on the ground is our choice. When you finally decide to pull yourself out of your depression and doldrums, *Blow a Bubble Not a Gasket* contains 101 suggestions you can use to airlift your spirits.

The book is divided into five sections, offering ideas for fun that enrich the total person. Most contain humorous stories about my friends and family. In some cases, the names have been changed. The "physical" section offers ideas to get our bodies moving. Physical inactivity can be exhausting. In this section, you'll discover ways to get your body in motion and have fun at the same time. Some of the suggestions involve a type of physical exercise while others just move us in the direction of doing something new.

The suggestions in the "social" section encourage us to share our lives with people. We are 30 times more likely to laugh if we are with other people. When we're alone, stress surrounds us like a heavy cloud; but when we're with friends, the cloud lifts and often evaporates.

The "mental" section of this book acknowledges the importance of relieving our minds of stress. After all, it is our thoughts that determine how stressful we view each experience in life to be. When we exercise the mind by filling it with positive thoughts, we leave less room for negative, stressful ones.

Some thoughts and experiences stir within us deep emotions. If those emotions are good, then stress is held at bay. The "emotional" section is developed with practical ideas for producing the emotions of happiness and optimism even when the circumstances are not favorable. Remember, emotions are a choice. No one can give them to us.

And finally, the "spiritual" section addresses the essence of who we are. We are a spirit, we have a soul, and we live in a body. If our spirit is distressed and discouraged, then true fun is out of our reach. The stories and information in the spiritual section refer specifically to my beliefs and experiences as a Christian. However, it is my prayer that this section will be a blessing to everyone who reads it, regardless of religious persuasion.

If you will, do me a favor. When you read this book, don't pass it along to a friend. Keep it and buy them another copy. Stress is relentless, like storms at sea. When the wind stops blowing and the waves subside, we rejoice. But as sure as big fish eat little ones, another storm will come. Be prepared! Keep a copy of *Blow a Bubble Not a Gasket* on your bookshelf. At the first sign of mounting stress, open the book and find a suggestion that works for you that day, that moment.

The question is sometimes asked, "What are you living for . . . ?" Some people live their lives to enrich their families, to succeed in their jobs, to reach some worthy goal, or to pursue and please their God. All of these can be noble reasons for living, but the wise person will never lose sight of the fact that life is worth living, just for the fun of it. We were not created to be miserable. If, in your pursuit of other goals, the surging tide of stress begins to bash and pulsate its way through your veins, remember the choice is yours. So, go blow a bubble, not a gasket!

SECTION I

PHYSICAL FUN

1

Blow bubbles!

When you feel like the pressures of life are upon you and you are about to blow a gasket, blow bubbles instead! Blowing bubbles is inexpensive fun. A big bottle usually costs less than two dollars, and with that simple investment, you can laugh for hours! Now doesn't that sound like more fun than succumbing to your stress?

I love adding fun to my life, and the lives of my friends and family, with simple things. One day while shopping with a friend at an outlet mall, we walked by a toy store. I casually asked if she wanted to go in, and she replied, "No. We don't need any toys." I was stopped in my tracks by the thought, "With the stressful schedules and challenges of our jobs, no two people ever needed to play more than we!" So in we went.

Prominently displayed near the checkout counter was an

old, familiar toy—bottles of bubble soap. We both bought a bottle, giggling as we paid for them.

That night we went out on my patio and blew bubbles! When the evening came to a close, my friend admitted that this was the most fun she had experienced in weeks.

Bubbles are pretty, light and fragile. Bubbles stay in motion, some going up and others down. We can create them, chase them and try to catch them. Don't burst my bubble. Buy some, and blow your own!

2

Explore a bookstore with a coffee shop.

You need not take part in an expensive outing or travel to an exotic location to have fun. Often the best times await you in ordinary places—like bookstores.

I've never been to a bookstore I couldn't get mentally and emotionally lost in. The very titles of most books are enough to whisk me off into a fantasyland of thoughts. Hours seem like minutes.

One of my favorite bookstores is Square Books in Oxford, Mississippi. The building is small, and two stories high. Tables, shelves, racks, trunks and staircases overflow with books and magazines covering every conceivable topic. Find a spot to relax and read among the benches, rocking chairs and stools scattered around. Should you doze off, don't worry, no one will say a word.

After your relaxing read, you can venture upstairs to a little counter where a variety of coffees, teas, sodas and pastries are served. Have a seat at one of the little tables arranged near a section of books written by Mississippi authors, or lounge at one of the tables lining a second-story balcony overlooking the town square. The friendly atmosphere has a down-home feel. The people are respectful and quiet, though periodically someone will laugh out loud, share a line from a book and others will join in. Square Books is a delightful place to be.

The same could be said for bookstores around the world. I tried to get lost in a bookstore in Paris, but the store didn't have quite the same effect for me. However, to the French it did! The idea is to find a place where humor thrives and go there. Visit a bookstore near you. Inside its doors lies a world of fun.

3

Skip!

When was the last time you skipped? Has it been a while? Somewhere between childhood and adulthood our natural enthusiasm settles down. As adults, we constantly face the task of keeping the child within us alive. One way to stir the child within you is to do a few childlike things from time to time. Skipping should be at the top of the list.

One day I was trying to entertain some children. The youngsters were skipping, so I joined them. Wow! Skipping down the road felt good. Predictably, I didn't skip far before getting out of step. When I first stumbled, I did the same thing the children did. I squealed! I felt foolish, but thrilled!

Skipping without smiling is almost impossible. Start in your own backyard. Invite a friend to join you. Laughing at and with each other is rejuvenating. Don't expect to go a long way. A little skipping consumes a lot of energy. I'm confident that someone has calculated the calories burned during this activity. However, skipping is not about getting exercise or burning calories or even playing with our children. It is about keeping the child that lives inside each of us alive. So skip! Don't forget to squeal!

4

Wear a costume.

Costumes are great for parties and are also helpful sources of fun in classrooms, businesses and anywhere people congregate.

For example, when Nancy discusses Shakespeare in her classroom, she wears Elizabethan costumes. Romeo's Juliet and Petrucio's Kathryn come to life before the students' eyes.

A friend of mine, who is a college science instructor in Kansas, introduces new lab experiments by dressing as The Amazing Tallenski with a cape draped on his shoulders and an artist's beret on his head. The charade guarantees student attention.

Another friend, Linda, has collected costumes all her life. No holiday finds her unadorned. Wherever she goes, the costumes demonstrate her zest for life.

Would your boss allow you to wear a costume? Have

you asked? Some employers prefer a formal atmosphere in the workplace. However, even professionals can coordinate colors with holiday events and wear cheerful ties.

Have you considered wearing a costume at home? You don't need permission in your own house. When you answer the door on Halloween night, why not surprise the children with your own rendition of Superman? I promise you will be the one who gets the treat!

5

Take a hike.

Hiking is fun! More than just a walk, hiking is getting a sweaty forehead, feeling the sun bathe your skin, sharing the experience with a friend, and adventuring into the unexplored.

A hike up Diamondhead remains a highlight of Dickie's and my honeymoon in Hawaii. Surprisingly, the mountain path was poorly marked, as though the state didn't want hundreds of people climbing to the top. We persevered. The path led to a legion of steps—I lost count somewhere around 50. At the top of the steps, we entered a dark tunnel. We felt our way along the wall of the tunnel until we reached an iron ladder that extended straight up the wall. The ladder led to a tiny exit hole at the top of the mountain.

As we emerged, we stood speechless. Okay, we were out of breath, but the view was absolutely awe-inspiring. In every direction, nature painted a masterpiece. We lingered there . . . chatting, laughing, sitting quietly. What an adventure.

Not all hiking trails lead up mountains. Some are in public parks. Others are through historic villages. Some follow train tracks and river beds. Others wind through neighborhood streets or big city blocks. So put on a comfortable pair of shoes, pick a route, and take a hike!

6

Finger paint.

Finger painting can breathe life into us at any age. Though physically you may live to be very old, if you remain mentally and emotionally young, you can be filled with a zest for living.

As a child, I loved finger painting; but, as I grew older, the paint seemed messy and it got under my nails. However, when my niece, Heather, came to visit me, I was more interested in having fun than staying clean. I purchased a finger painting kit, and Heather and I created an afternoon of sheer fun. We each fingered our way through a dozen pictures, all in the modern art category without one recognizable tree.

Amazingly, the masterpieces were actually pretty and cheerful. We used bright colors: red, yellow, purple, blue, green and orange. Looking at the elementary art long after

Heather had flown home, I vividly remembered the fun we shared painting each picture.

I still don't like to get paint under my nails, but I love a good laugh. I wonder what the finished product would look like if I wore gloves? With or without gloves, dive in. Let your fingers do the walking through the . . . yellow paint! Paint yourself some fun!

7

Sleep in a different bed.

Sleep in a hammock in your backyard. Cuddle with your children in the tree house. Be creative. If nothing else, put your pillows at the foot of the bed. Once you are asleep, where or what the bed is probably won't make any difference. However, those critical moments when we quiet our minds for sleep can be greatly enhanced by a new location. Our subconscious can be stimulated. Humor can be released from the prison of "sameness."

My house has two bedrooms available for guests. One is equipped with a queen-sized bed, and the other one has a queen-sized sleeper sofa. After several occasions when both rooms were required, I worried that the sofa did not provide a good night's sleep. I feared those guests might feel somewhat slighted. To test it, I insisted that Dickie and I spend the night on the sleeper.

Once we settled in, our talkative mood turned to giggles. We watched a little TV in the dark room, snuggled and the next thing I knew, it was morning. We decided the sleeper was fine, but more valuable was the new idea for fun we discovered. On our next trip to the sofa, we'll take popcorn.

8

Tour your hometown.

Located near almost every town in America is a place worth touring—a pickle factory, horse ranch, scenic overlook, novelty shop . . . something. These special places offer fun dished up in a variety of forms, but few local people utilize them. We travel across the country to see points of interest and often neglect fascinating places near home. A simple phone call to obtain admission prices, location and hours of operation, along with a short drive may be all it takes to start the good times rolling.

When my family lived in southern California, my visits there often included touring Disneyland, Knotts Berry Farm and Laguna Beach. When they moved to northern California, visits included San Francisco's major points of interests and the Napa Valley Wine Country. Once I returned home, however, I settled into the mundane, never visiting the many points of interest in my own town.

Then one day my niece came to visit. Though Gulfport, Mississippi, has little that can compare to Disneyland, I decided to show her my town. For the first time in 25 years, I toured Beauvoir, the stately last home of the Confederacy's only president, Jefferson Davis. We ambled through the rooms of the house, reading captions under pictures, uniforms and weapons. We walked quietly through the cemetery on the grounds with its graves of Confederate soldiers. I took my niece's picture by a big column on the front porch that overlooks the Gulf of Mexico. A whole afternoon was gone in a flash. The outing was fun, relaxing, and educational, and was only a short drive from my neighborhood.

Since then, I've discovered college campuses, local businesses, and City Halls welcome the public. Some towns have zoos and museums, art galleries and gardens, parks and campgrounds, all eager to entertain.

Don't wait until vacation time to tour the highlights of someone else's hometown. Start today and appreciate the wonders in your own backyard.

9

Juggle.

Can you juggle? If not, it's time you learned! Juggling is universally pleasing. Clowns and jesters have dazzled crowds for centuries with their dexterity. People everywhere find the gravity-defying objects intriguing. Juggling gets you active, keeps your hands busy and takes your mind off more mundane issues.

Many years ago, I accepted a part in a community theater play. The demands of mastering my role included learning to juggle. So, between classes, in my office, in the halls and in the courtyard, everywhere I went I juggled. People constantly stopped and asked me what I was doing, but what they really wanted to know was why I was juggling and if they could give it a try! Finally, after six weeks of practice, I still could not complete the entire five-minute routine required by the play without dropping a ball.

However, I am still grateful for the experience. I met wonderful people, had lots of fun and semi-learned a new skill.

Juggling is not just an activity for the theater. Classrooms can benefit from the fun, too. If students are falling asleep on you, start juggling. With a little imagination, you can turn "facts" into a game and toss them in the air. In business offices, coffee breaks provide an ideal opportunity to practice the jester's art. The physical movement of the activity can be as stimulating as caffeine. Hospitals and hotels, factories and fisheries, playgrounds and parking lots are all juggling-friendly. Remove the breakables and get started. Small, homemade beanbags make great objects to toss because they are inexpensive (should one go down a hole) and they don't bounce. Be careful with bowling pins.

Once you begin to master the art of juggling, don't lose sight of your goal—have fun! If you allow yourself to become discouraged with your progress, you are missing the point. Juggling provides many delightful moments. Enjoy it!

10

Make homemade ice cream.

Do you remember the last time you had real homemade ice cream? No, the half-gallon from the local grocery store just isn't the same. I mean creamy, made-from-scratch ice cream.

I remember my mother making vanilla ice cream on the stove. She would cook the milk, eggs, sugar and flavoring, then pour the mixture into ice trays and place them in the freezer. A few hours later, heaven manifested itself on earth in the form of a huge bowl of hard vanilla ice cream!

The day my daddy brought home our first hand-cranked ice cream freezer was a day for celebrating. We followed the instructions carefully, placing the ingredients in the canister and the canister inside the wooden tub. Next, we alternately placed rock salt and ice in the tub until it was full. Last, we draped a towel over the top of the tub, and Daddy slowly turned the crank. Everybody wanted a turn. I could only help a little because the ice cream quickly became too hard for me. Then Daddy would let me sit on top of the tub while he turned the crank. At last, we removed the lid and beheld a canister full of fluffy, creamy ice cream!

As a young, single adult, furnishing my own kitchen, I purchased an ice cream freezer . . . the hand-cranked kind. I was strong enough to go the distance with the machine. I used a mix, added condensed milk, sat on my small apartment patio, and turned and turned the handle.

Make your own homemade ice cream. You're sure to crank up some fun!

11

Switch roles for a day.

Want to have fun, Mom? Let your children tell you what to do for a day.

Want a new perspective, Mr. Superintendent? Switch roles with a high school senior for a day. Yes, you must attend his or her classes!

How about you, Mr. Executive? Why don't you switch places with your foreman? You watch the line and let the foreman work on one of your projects.

Pastor, let your secretary attend the conference, and you answer the phone and type the church bulletin.

As absurd as this may sound, the results can be rewarding.

The college where I teach selected a new public speaking textbook which I was required to use in my communications class. Time was an issue. When was I going to read it?

I decided not to read it. I decided to let my students study the textbook and tell me what was in it. In teaching their chapters, the students were instructed not to succumb to any of the complaints they normally had about teachers, such as boring tone of voice, distracting mannerisms, being poorly prepared and lacking class involvement.

The results of the assignment were thrilling for the students and me. Most had never been asked to formally teach anything. Some felt humbled by the task. Three of the students enjoyed teaching the class so much they changed their majors to pursue education degrees. And what were my benefits? I had a wonderful opportunity to evaluate their oral communication skills; plus, I became familiar with the textbook at no extra time cost to me.

Attitude is everything, so approach the opportunity positively. You will not only get a much-needed break from your routine, but you will also become more sensitive to other peoples' needs. Try it.

12

Dance!

Come on! Don't just stand there, grab a fun-loving partner and get moving! Don't worry; you don't have to dance like Fred Astaire and Ginger Rogers, or a Rockette, unless you are getting paid for it. Fun-filled dancing energizes the body and soul.

You can dance anywhere. As a teenager, I learned to rock 'n roll in my living room, holding on to the door handle for a partner. As a teacher, I danced in my classroom! When answers were slow in coming, I'd break into a shuffle-ball-change, much to the delight of my students. Sometimes now, when I'm standing in a slow grocery store line, I'll start to sway, then step back and forth, then hum a few bars. I'm dancing, and I've just made myself feel better!

When you dance to a musical beat, you become syn-chronized with a life force that enlivens you. You work in opposition to static gravity that holds you captive to the earth. As you dance, you'll experience freedom with every twist and turn, bend and dip, step and leap. And though your feet seem always to return to the floor, your spirits soar, rising higher and higher with the steady flow of the beat.

Sunbeams dance on water. Flowers sway on stems. Hearts beat in rhythm. Pendulums swing in clocks. Moving to a beat is natural. Embrace the rhythm of life. DANCE!

13

Search for treasure.

One man's junk is another man's treasure. Though finding your treasure in an expensive specialty shop can be fun, the happiness of an expensive purchase cannot compare to the thrill of the unexpected find by the avid yard sale shopper. Like true miners, sifting through dirt and discovering gold brings exhilaration. Mere mortals have beaten the system!

One Saturday morning, during a visit to my aunt's house in Kansas, her alarm clock rang at 6 a.m. "Get up, little Jane. We're going to some yard sales today." Though yard sales had never been of particular interest to me, she seemed excited about it, so I eagerly joined her.

By 7 a.m. we were in the car, newspaper in hand, plotting the order of the stops we would make. The first house had mainly clothes, so we didn't spend much time there. At the second stop, my aunt purchased fruit canning jars and small, clay flower pots for a nickel each. At our third and last stop, two boxes of books, mostly novels, attracted my aunt. Her total charge for three books was $1.50. I found two brass candle holders with interesting rose-shaped bases. I realized a little polishing would turn them into charming coffee table items. The owner asked $4 for the pair; but, after I told her I was taking them all the way to Mississippi, she cut the cost in half!

My aunt and I returned home by 9 a.m., cooked breakfast and laughed and giggled about our finds. Though many years have passed since that visit, my $2 brass candleholders still sit proudly on my coffee table.

Set your alarm clock, plot your course and set out to find your own "buried" treasure!

14

Declare a special occasion.

Valentine's Day is the day we celebrate love by exchanging cards and giving chocolate candy. On patriotic days, we celebrate our freedom and proudly fly American flags and wear red, white, and blue. Why wait for a holiday to celebrate? Why not declare an ordinary day to be a special occasion and dress and act accordingly?

Declare today special and wear a corsage; or, give a corsage to a fellow worker, proclaiming them to be King or Queen for the day. Invite a friend to lunch. Go to your favorite restaurant and order appetizers, desserts, the works! After all, today is a special day. Who declared it to be so? You did!

You can turn any ordinary day or project into something

special. Two nights before my wedding, my Aunt Mable did that very thing. In all the hustle, we had forgotten rice bags. No one really had time to make them, but my aunt assumed the responsibility. She bought the supplies and went to work. Several hours later, when I entered the room, I burst into laughter, as did my mom and dad. With ribbon draped around her neck, a bucket of rice between her legs and netting piled on the kitchen table, there my precious aunt sat, wearing a housecoat and the elegant new yellow hat she had purchased to wear for my wedding. She looked at us and said, "I'm modeling the latest fashion for rice bag parties. Want to join me?" We all needed that laugh.

Declare a National Postcard Day and send some to friends. Institute a Fabulous Friday Day and set-off fireworks with neighbors. Celebrate the invention of computers and place bows on all the monitors in the office.

An occasion is made special by the attitudes and imaginations of the people who embrace it. Since it's your choice, why not declare today to be Blow A Bubble Day. Celebrate by blowing bubbles or chewing bubble gum or soaking in a bubble bath. Bubble up some fun.

15

Experiment with exotic foods.

Think about the times you pass through the fruit and vegetable displays in your local grocery store. In a rush, you select familiar items like carrots, onions and apples, leaving in the bins wonderful objects of humor like bok choy, leeks, Jamaica cactus peas and star fruit.

Next time you're in the produce section, buy an unusual fruit or vegetable. When you add something out of the ordinary to your list, grocery shopping, cooking and serving the food all become fun and adventurous.

One of my favorite encounters with an unusual vegetable was at an arts and crafts festival in Vermont where I first laid eyes on a purple potato. These potatoes were purple, not mauve or dark brown or slightly tinted . . . PURPLE.

Purple potatoes may be commonplace to you, but not to me. I gave in to curiosity and bought a bag. After I returned home, I sparingly gave the potatoes as gifts to special people. Left with only three, I never cooked them. They rotted in my refrigerator. To this day, I have no idea how a purple potato tastes or looks when cooked.

Each time you experiment with something different, you open the door to a new world. Admittedly, some of the doors

are quickly closed, like the Tofu door was for me, but others are entered, explored and enjoyed. I can guarantee, if I ever see another purple potato, I'm cooking that spud!

16

Coach.

If you possess a love for young people, the ability to positively encourage others, and a belief in the team concept, you can coach a youth league ball team. You don't have to be a parent. You don't even need experience. You should, however, be prepared to laugh frequently!

At age six, my niece Heather became eligible for youth soccer and softball teams. Her dad, J., walked Heather to her first soccer practice and was drafted to be an assistant coach on the spot, though he had never touched a soccer ball before! He soon became the coach of her soccer team and her softball team. Her mom, Sandy, filled the positions of manager and statistician. Sports became a family affair. They made new friends and taught Heather and her friends how to follow rules, be responsible, play fair and win and lose like champions.

Don't lose sight of the fun in this civic activity. In good faith, you can laugh at and with the children. Laugh as little Libby runs toward the wrong goal and Tommy's pants fall to his ankles while running to home plate. Chuckle as Johnny gets to first base for the first time and calls back to you, "What do I do now?" Shout for joy with Susie when she catches her first fly ball in the outfield and manages to hold on to it, and with Bonnie when she finally connects with her first header, and with Billy when he scores his first goal.

Money can't buy this kind of fun, but working with youth league ball teams can.

17

Rediscover the coloring book.

You may remember the pride you felt when you won first place in the school's art contest, or that special feeling when you gave one of your early paintings to your parents, and they displayed it on the refrigerator. I don't share these memories. My houses were always lopsided. Teachers thought my dogs were cows, and my raindrops were big warts.

A few years ago, my mother was in the hospital recovering from hip surgery, and I grew bored sitting in her room. I ventured to the gift shop and bought a coloring book. While my mother slept, I colored. The time flew by and Mom was out of the hospital before I finished the coloring book.

The book didn't go to waste. Anytime I was sitting for a long period of time, waiting for something or traveling, I would take the coloring book out of my bag and start to color. What a conversation starter! I met the nicest people, all fascinated by the fact that an adult was coloring in a book.

I still don't draw much, though I have tried to upgrade my doodling. My raindrops have improved, but my dogs still look like cows. However, fun is not about talent. "Fun" is about being smart enough to see the humor in everything, even our inability to paint and draw. If you need a good laugh, and your art is as weak as mine, play with a coloring book and laugh at yourself. No harm is done, and many benefits are gained.

18

Relocate.

Think about the activities you do repeatedly. Now think about the location of these activities. Where do you plan your presentations, research your case, grade your papers, read to your children, paint your nails? Where do you drink your morning coffee or eat your evening meals? Relocate! A new environment for an old activity creates a fresh experience and adds spice to life.

Though I understand and proclaim the benefits of change, when I was a teacher, I secretly preferred that things remain the same in my classroom. I stood to teach, while the students sat to learn. However, when springtime arrived, the students' always appealed to have class under the trees. The request was difficult to refuse. Once seated in the shade with the breeze blowing, the class discussions seemed livelier. Time flew.

I recall when I was a child, each night my daddy read the evening newspaper in his favorite recliner in the den. Occasionally, he moved to a front porch rocker. Before long, I would join him with a book, and my brother would ask for the sports section. We perched on that porch until Mom called us for supper. Those moments of peaceful fun are still precious in my memory. For some reason they never occurred in the den.

There are advantages to predictability and consistency; however, fun and creativity are not among them. Those characteristics thrive on uniqueness and spontaneity.

So the next time someone accuses you of barking up the wrong tree, quit barking and climb it! The world looks different from the top of a tree!

19

Smell the roses.

Root yourself to a fond memory in nature. Petunias, magnolias or a barrel cactus might work best for you. Periodically, stop and admire it, photograph it, talk about it.

When my mother came to live with Dickie and me, she brought from her home more than just furniture and clothes. She brought her rose bushes. These were not just any common roses. No! These rose bushes were over 100 years old.

Forty-five years earlier, Mother had transplanted, at her new home, cuttings from rose bushes from her childhood home. Taking those roses with us to my house was the only option. But this time, a cutting from the bushes wouldn't do. She wanted the root system.

I began to dig and soon discovered why roses bloom all summer, in spite of the heat. The root system goes down deep into the soil, DEEP. Mother laughed at me as I dug and said she'd never seen me work so hard. I wasn't laughing. I was hot and not at all sure I was ever going to find the end of those roots. Just as I was about to chop off the roots and yank the bushes from the ground, my friend Wilbur happened by. He finished the task and loaded the bushes in our car.

Thankfully, transplanting our old beauties into the new yard was much easier. Mother's green thumb worked its magic once again, and the bushes flourished.

The roses will always be a special reminder of the time my mother spent living with me. I'll remember their history, which is my history, too. I'll remember the day we struggled to up-root them. What a day! Each spring I expect to smell those roses and laugh about it again.

Friends and family will come and go, but nature can accompany us to the end. Every rose reminds me of Mom and I smile.

20

Browse a toy store.

The perfect place to re-establish your connection to the child within is a toy store. Let's take an imaginary shopping spree.

The first aisle showcases the latest playthings for infants: rings to chew, soft balls to grasp and colorful mobiles to dance over beds. I like the mobile with stars, moons, clouds and angels hanging from it. I'll buy that one. You pick something, too.

The second aisle displays items for young children: dump trucks, tricycles, baby dolls and playhouses. I like mini furniture, so I'll get the playhouse and start a collection of tiny chairs and little tables. What are you going to buy?

The third aisle contains toys for pre-adolescent children, offering the boys GI Joes and machine guns that shoot soft darts. For girls, this aisle displays bride dolls, large hook-and-eye sewing kits and hula-hoops. Since my waistline needs constant work, I'll take the hula-hoop. You choose something, too.

Stuffed animals of every size and description fill the fourth aisle. I'll take the teddy bear that reminds me of one I had when I was six. He was black and white and about two feet tall. I called him Teddy. Original! I think I'll name this one Teddy, too. What are you going to name your animal?

Board games, bicycles, Ping-Pong tables and sporting equipment claim space in the remaining aisles. I'm still reeling from my encounter with a weird game I purchased for my niece, so I will pick the familiar croquet set. What will you choose?

Just thinking about your favorite toys is fun, and it doesn't cost anything to visit a toy store. Let the child within out!

21

Take time to watch a funny movie.

How often do you mutter the phrase, "I just don't have enough time"? The thought steals peace and joy from you, establishing a mindset of hurry, frustration, and lack of control. Instead of letting those feelings control you, relax, sit back and watch a funny movie!

At the end of a long week of finding myself saying over and over again, "I don't have time," a friend invited me to a movie. I didn't have time to go . . . really! But why didn't I have time? The person who invited me had a job and family, too. I decided to accept the invitation. My first laugh came within minutes of the movie starting. Then, on and off for more than an hour, I smiled, giggled and sometimes laughed out loud. The whole excursion cost me no more than two hours, and I returned home totally refreshed.

Too tired to go out? Finances too limited for a movie outing? Then opt to rent a video instead—the funnier the better! Curl up on your favorite, comfortable couch or recliner and start the movie. The relaxing experience will rest the body and refresh the mind.

Often stress is self-imposed. You must stop and enjoy some fun along the way or you will miss out on much of the joy in life. Take the time to watch a funny movie!

22

Spend the night away from home.

To relieve some of the stress that comes with traveling, or simply to take a break from your own household responsibilities, make a reservation and spend the night in a bed and breakfast inn. Unlike hotels, which tend to be carbon copies of one another, each bed and breakfast offers a unique lodging experience. Each provides the comforts of home with the advantage of having someone else to cook and clean.

For years, one of my and Dickie's favorites was Isom Place, the home of Mrs. Opal Worthy in Oxford, Mississippi. Isom Place was an antebellum house with large rooms and high ceilings. Each guest was warmly greeted on a porch adorned with tall, white columns and then given a guided tour through the house.

Breakfast at Isom Place was served around a large mahogany dining table. Guests would often linger at the table after breakfast and enjoy conversation and coffee. When Mrs. Worthy, because of failing health, sold Isom Place, she welcomed several of her "regulars" into her newly acquired four-bedroom house. We accepted the invitation because, after all, we had become family.

We also stayed in a bed and breakfast in London once. Our bedroom was on the third floor of the house, our bathroom was on the second floor, and breakfast was served in the basement! As unlikely as it sounds, we had fun running up and down the narrow staircase. Each morning the owners would recommend which subways to take and the best places to visit. We felt at home abroad.

Bed and breakfast accommodations are located in small and large towns, resort villages and throughout the countryside. There's one near you now, and at least one on the way to where you are going. To relieve stress and have fun, too, step out of your world and into theirs for a night, a weekend, or longer. Fun waits behind each unique door.

23

Cheer the home team.

Cheers, chants and chuckles await you in the bleachers of your neighborhood high school stadium. You don't have to love football or basketball or any of the spectator sports. You only need to fall in step with those who do—people like the local pastor, mayor, grocer, mailman, beautician, insurance salesman, nurse and gardener. Their enthusiasm for the game will energize you.

As a high school teacher, I went regularly to home games. My comments on Monday mornings seemed important to the students who participated. "Jimmy, you did a great job at the game. That opening play was unbelievable!" "Rita, I loved your trumpet solo in the band." Or, to the child who simply supported the team's efforts from the stands, I would say, "Robert, I saw you at the game. You looked like you were having a great time." What I said to them didn't seem to matter as much as the fact that I noticed they were there.

Though no longer a full-time teacher and now removed from the high school setting, I still occasionally go to high school games. I continue to feel a kinship to the school, the community and the people.

A word of caution: While the team is driving for a tie goal in the final moments on the clock, keep your blood pressure down. Remember, the sport is only a game. Also, take a cushion with you. Wooden bleachers have splinters!

24

Play with a puppet.

Hand puppets can bring joy wherever you are. Visitors to hospitals and nursing homes use them to cheer the sick and confined. Babysitters pass the time telling stories with puppets. Children create make-believe friends with them.

With just a little imagination, you can find a fun use for a puppet, regardless of your profession. I once agreed to speak about conflict resolution to an entire fifth grade at an elementary school. While preparing for the speech, I wondered, "How do you dress for a fifth-grade audience? How can I be sure I've geared the complex material for the fifth-grade mind?" Then I remembered working with the puppet ministry at church. Producing the movements and voices for the furry little hand-held creatures was fun. In those audiences, even the adults laughed! I made up my mind. Somehow, I would work a puppet into the presentation.

I selected a large, blue, fuzzy puppet and named him Huey. The presentation began with Huey crying profusely because someone called him a name. The insult hurt his feelings and made him angry. He wanted to get even; he wanted to fight. The ensuing conversation involved the students discussing ways to handle the problem other than fighting. The presentation earned accolades from principals, teachers and students. The puppet saved the day.

You can find puppets at toy stores and specialty shops. You can even make one out of materials such as socks, paper bags and scraps of material.

My only advice, start lifting weights and exercising your hands now, because your muscles will be sore after your first few puppet practices. Don't worry, your hands will eventually strengthen, as will your sense of humor.

25

Rearrange your furniture.

Look at the rooms in your house or office. How long has your desk faced that door, the chair sat in that corner or the bookcase braced that wall? Isn't it time for a change?

I covered most of the floors in my home with orange carpet. Looking at the carpet from one direction, the pile appeared dark orange. From the other direction, the pile appeared peach. The carpet made the room vibrant. However, time became the enemy of my beloved carpet. Frequently used walking areas soon became dark pathways glaringly contrasted between light unused areas. To lengthen the life of the carpet, I needed to periodically re-route traffic by rearranging the furniture.

Little did I know what an adventure in fun rearranging

furniture would be. What I accomplished went far beyond saving the carpet. A fresh, expectant air permeated each newly designed living room. Things were different. We, as strange as it seems, were different.

You can experience a similar feeling by simply rearranging pictures on the wall or placing new flowers in a vase. Changing even small things in your environment can make a difference in your outlook and add a great deal of subtle fun to your life.

26

Monkey around.

Playgrounds are designed with one thought in mind—fun. Even if your agility on the equipment has diminished with age, don't let that stop you. Take a trip to your local playground and swing, slide and dare to dangle from the monkey bars.

Though Dickie and I have a spacious backyard, our Italian Greyhound, Gucci, is still unable to run in it at full speed. Conveniently, an elementary school with a large playground is located down the street from our house.

The first afternoon we walked Gucci to the school to let him run, we entertained ourselves on the playground equipment. Sitting in the swings brought back great memories of elementary school. After reminiscing awhile, we grew dizzy from swinging, so we moved to the monkey bars.

As children we were both good at throwing our legs over

the monkey bars and swinging upside down. Now, decades later, we were content to leap up to a tall bar and hang from our hands.

As we walked back to our house, all three tongues were hanging out—Gucci's, Dickie's and mine. We were giggling, though, and we didn't seem as tired as when we started. The outing took about 20 minutes, didn't cost a dime and provided some of the best fun we had all week.

What are you waiting for? Visit a playground near you. Go ahead! "Monkey-around" a little!

27

Start a collection.

Do you know someone who collects things like model trains, dolls, thimbles or old cameras? Did you notice the twinkle in their eyes and the joy in their voice as they told you about each item? Want to feel that kind of joy? Start your own collection!

People who visit my home are drawn to my refrigerator. Rather than opening the door, guests stand and stare at my collection of magnets that cover the whole front of the refrigerator. Each magnet reminds me of a special time or a beautiful place. I have a ceramic snowflake from Keystone, Colorado, an acrylic leaf from Vermont, a dried pepper from San Antonio, and a mask from The Phantom of the Opera, just to name a few. I collect magnets, and for me, magnets collect joy.

A friend of mine collects pin-on, tin badges, also called

buttons. She wears a different one every day. Sometimes she wears one on her collar. At other times she pins one to her sleeve, belt, back, leg, shoe or chain. Most of the badges display funny slogans, and all encourage positive thoughts and good feelings.

Collect something that you enjoy . . . books, buckets, rolling pins, T-shirts . . . anything. Just start collecting. Then share your treasures with others. Collections are a wonderful source of fun.

28

Smile!

Sitting right where you are, smile. Go on. Smile! How do you feel? Did you sense a slight lift in your spirit when you smiled? The difference in the way it makes you feel is amazing!

Norman Cousins, in *The Anatomy of an Illness,* tells us that laughter stimulates the production of endorphins and antibodies, creating a feeling of good health. The simple act of smiling accomplishes the very same thing on a smaller scale.

As an added benefit, smiling reduces wrinkles! Thirteen facial muscles are used to smile, while 78 are needed to frown. If a wrinkle were going to be left in a place where we bend our face, wouldn't it be nice if the wrinkle were in the shape of a smile?

Smiling is a universal language. While we were in Hawaii, my husband Dickie and I took an evening dinner cruise. We were seated at a large table with a couple from

Japan, a couple from France and two students from Argentina. Beyond a few simple words, none of them spoke English; however, we laughed, smiled and nodded our heads in agreement all evening, feeling certain that we had communicated. We had fun that evening.

Smiling says a lot about us. The upward turned corner of our lips tells people that we are receptive, confident or in a good mood. The gesture makes people comfortable in our presence. So be quick to smile. Start those endorphins flowing!

SECTION II

SOCIAL FUN

29

Bake cookies. Give them away.

What a simple thing a cookie is, but what a delicious source of joy. You don't have to be a gourmet chef to bake them. You can purchase already prepared cookie dough from any grocery store. It's the thought that counts when you brighten someone's day with a fresh baked cookie.

After church one night, our Sunday school class was invited to Joy's home for a fellowship. Music wasn't the only thing that filled the air. The wonderful scent of home-baked cookies was maddening—only because Joy didn't offer the cookies to us right away. Uppermost in everyone's mind were the questions "Where are the cookies? When can we have them?"

Finally, after what seemed like an eternity, Joy spoke the

magic words, "Would anyone like some refreshments?" The line around the table quickly formed. A dozen different kinds of homemade cookies spread before us, some boasting chocolate chips, while others flaunted nuts, cinnamon, sugar coatings and candied fruit.

As I sampled my way around the table, I discovered the sweetest recipe of all. Joy began telling me about how much she and her mom loved to bake cookies. The fun doesn't stop for Joy and her mom in the baking process. The greatest pleasure comes when they give the cookies away.

Elderly shut-ins live in Joy's neighborhood, and on holidays, she and her mom deliver cookies to them. Once, when Joy had not arrived by the usual time, a neighbor called to inquire if she was sick and to ask about the cookies.

When it comes to giving cookies away, the thought is really the only thing that counts. The feelings derived are predictable—gratitude and fun! Friendships created by the gesture are guaranteed.

30

Tell jokes.

Eight-year-old Susie was crazy about school, while her six-year-old sister was less enthusiastic. "Let's play school," suggested Susie one day. "All right," agreed the younger sister grudgingly, "but let's pretend I'm absent today." Though only a joke, I know how the six-year-old felt.

Opportunities for using jokes are boundless, and the added humor helps you survive many situations.

Parenting teenagers, for example, requires that you learn to see the humor in chaos. Did you hear about the scheme one father devised to get his teenage son to clean his room? The father just throws the keys to the family car into the room once a week!

Boring memos challenge both supervisors and employees. Spice it up! Sprinkle jokes and humorous sayings throughout the writing.

Instead of telling your aunt about the weather and your work, write to her about a funny thing the children said or a joke you heard this morning on the radio. The re-telling of the "funny" will delight both you and your aunt.

Jokes make any place more cheerful. Always keep one or two of them handy for times when conversation lulls or tension runs high. Remember to tell only clean and wholesome jokes. Your character, after all, is at stake.

31

Dine with friends.

Sometimes in our quest for fun we overlook the obvious. If I had to name the social activity I enjoy the most, dinner out with friends would be my answer. I have hundreds of memories of meals spent in exotic restaurants and greasy, small cafes. If you want to improve your fun quotient, serve it up with dinner.

I visit my friend Wanda as often as I can. Ninety miles separate us, so generally our visits are only for an afternoon. We don't want to waste a minute of our time together cooking or washing dishes, so out the door we go to any one of a dozen restaurants that awaits us.

Dinner out doesn't have to be elaborate or expensive. Karen and Don live in our same town, but getting together with them is challenging. Distance isn't the problem as much as schedules. We generally have to plan our times together far in advance.

One night Dickie and I were at home with nothing pressing to do. On a whim, we picked up the phone and called Karen and Don. Miraculously, their evening was free, too. We drove to their house and the four of us headed for a local fast food restaurant. The outing was totally stress-free. We

 didn't worry whether the meal was in our budgets. We just relaxed and enjoyed the company.

Dinner with friends is a great source of joy! Make your reservations now.

32

Choose a mascot.

A mascot is anything that represents the character and spirit of a unit. It becomes a tangible focal point for the affection one has for the unit itself. Every home, office, classroom or team should have one. Even when we fail, our mascot is there to remind us that we stand for something bigger than our failure.

During World War II, pilots and crews gave their planes names. Pictures painted onto the sides of the planes represented those names. Before entering the plane, a flyer would kiss the picture or slap it, and hop aboard. The picture became the crew's mascot. It stood for the affection the crew had developed for each other and their "bird." The mascot symbolized the spirit of that unit.

Dickie and I cheer for The University of Mississippi—the Ole Miss Rebels. The school's mascot is Colonel Reb, a tall caricature of a soldier dressed in a military uniform. On occasions, when the team is behind and they lose the ball, fans get depressed and frustrated. With "time out" on the field, Colonel Reb comes to the rescue!

He saunters out to the 50-yard line, dragging his feet and hanging his head, looking as depressed as the fans. Then, a look of mischief comes across his countenance. He spies a well-placed opponent's cheerleader with a football tucked under her arm. Colonel Reb tiptoes up to the cheerleader, steals the ball, and a chase ensues. The crowd roars. Will he score? Both sides are cheering, one for Colonel Reb, one for the cheerleader. With only inches to spare, Colonel Reb plunges toward the goal line and scores. The fans are ecstatic. Even if we lose the game, we won the race. Our mascot has saved the day!

We all need something to periodically remind us of our "unit's" spirit. When Johnny finishes with his Linus blanket, don't throw it away. Drape it over the kitchen broom and tie a ribbon around it. That blanketed broom could become the best mascot your family ever had.

33

Visit senior citizens.

All the face lifts, cosmetics, and fitness programs in the world cannot eradicate the effects of time. If you live long enough, you'll become a senior citizen—a person full of wisdom learned in the rigorous school of life with wonderful stories actually lived out in colorful details. For fantastic fun fit for all ages, visit a senior citizen.

One Sunday morning at Bible study the Mission Chairman asked all members to "adopt" a shut-in, a senior citizen that is homebound. We were to visit that person, mail cards or deliver gifts on holidays, and when possible, call them for a chat. I volunteered. As I read through the list of senior citizens, a pang pierced my heart. Mrs. Kracker's name was on the list.

Mrs. Kracker, known dearly as "Kracker" to most members, had been attending our church for more than 40 years.

She had worked as the church secretary and with the youth. Year after year, Kracker faithfully sat on the front pews during Sunday morning worship, but eventually, arthritis made movement difficult for her to attend, and she stayed home. Dickie and I agreed to adopt Kracker.

A friend who knew her well encouraged me to take lunch to Kracker on Christmas Day, as she wasn't expecting company until early evening. When my lunch guests had left, I packed containers of food into a box and off I went. The time I spent with Kracker flew by. We had fun. I brought her up to date about the church, and she told me about her family and her favorite baseball team, the Atlanta Braves, recounting many of their statistics and trades. Though Santa Claus had left me several gifts under the tree, the best gift I received that Christmas was the joy of my afternoon visit with Mrs. Kracker.

Senior citizens aren't always found on shut-in lists or in rocking chairs. You might have to chase some of them down on golf courses. You'll find others running civic organizations, campaigning for candidates or traveling to exotic places. One thing is for sure, wherever you find a senior citizen, you'll find a fun-loving experience close at hand.

34

Put a jigsaw puzzle together.

Do you need a reason to invite friends over? Is an evening out just not in the budget? Buy an inexpensive jigsaw puzzle or make your own puzzle by enlarging photographs and cutting them into pieces. Then pop some corn and invite your friends over. A few may be skeptical at first, but your enthusiasm for the puzzle will catch on.

Some of my favorite Christmas memories from childhood are the years when my Aunt Mable, along with my uncle and cousins, came to my house for the holidays. What joyous and chaotic occasions those Christmases were!

Beyond cooking and hiding gifts, uppermost in the adults' minds was how to keep the children occupied and out of trouble. A puzzle was the perfect solution! My brother, cousins and I would gather around a beautiful Duncan Phyfe, mahogany card table and squeal, chat, laugh and play until bedtime.

One of the nicest things about having fun with puzzles is that playing with them teaches us about life on a deeper level. For instance, we spend much of our time trying to put the pieces of our lives together. Early in the game, we discover the broad outlines of who we are, but often take years to determine where the smaller pieces of attitudes and dreams fit. Like selecting the right puzzle, in life we must select careers, hobbies and mates that truly interest us if we are to fully enjoy them. When these areas of our lives become difficult, our desire to see them completed will sustain us. We will continue to piece these areas together.

Occasionally, you may discover a couple of pieces are missing. Resist the urge to abandon the puzzle. Instead, find a small picture of yourself, cut it to fit the empty space and glue it in place. After all, we usually complete our work if we put ourselves into it and give it our all.

35

Share your talents.

What are your talents? Can you cook, sew, make bookmarks, write poetry or sing? Share your talents with someone else.

In order to meet someone other than a female in my college dormitory, I had to "hang out" in the lobby. Men were not allowed in the dorm rooms. Neither were televisions. So the lobby really wasn't a bad place to be.

Frequently, a young man in a wheel chair interrupted the routine of watching TV and flirting. Everyone knew Eddie. He played a mean folk guitar. I don't remember him ever telling a joke, and I don't think he dated any of the girls in the dorm. However, we all loved Eddie. When his music filled our lobby, so did singing, joy and fellowship.

I know a history teacher who is great at sketching portraits. While students are testing, he sits and sketches three or four thoughtful faces, depending on the length of the test. When students turn in their papers, he hands them the sketches. By the end of the semester, he has sketched all of his students and given each a signed picture. He's known as a hard teacher, but his history classes are always full.

I was speaking to a group of senior citizens once, feeling pleased about the good deed I was performing. Little did I know that the best deed was occurring in the seat before me. I noticed a gentleman busy with his hands, but I couldn't tell what he was doing. At the end of the program, he thanked me and handed me a flamingo, whittled from a

stick. People gathered around us to see the clever art. We laughed and complimented his work. Everyone has long since forgotten my speech, but I still have the flamingo.

Whatever your talent, use it. Someone will surely enjoy it. It's worth a try.

36

Welcome new neighbors with food.

When someone moves into your neighborhood, give them the gift of food. Casseroles and homemade bread are good. Preserves or pickles you canned yourself are thoughtful. A fruit basket, fresh vegetables or a baked ham can fill the bill. And don't forget the power of chocolate. Food shared symbolizes more than just a gift. Mankind must have food to live. A gift of something edible is an invitation "to live here," to put your roots down and make it your home.

Dickie and I never expected a visit so soon after moving into our first home. Boxes were stacked in every room, and I was locating places for things to "live" when the doorbell rang. I hurried to the door, and there stood Martha with a casserole. She greeted me warmly and welcomed me to the neighborhood. She reasoned that I probably did not have my kitchen unpacked, and that I would appreciate a break from fast foods. Though the cleaned casserole dish has long since been returned, I still cherish Martha's kindness.

The Bible, in Matthew 7:12b (NLT) says, "Do for others what you would like them to do for you." Knowing how much the casserole meant to us, I decided to pass the fun on when more new neighbors arrived. I didn't time it as well as Martha did. Terry's kitchen was fully functioning; though, by the look on her face, I knew my casserole was met with equal appreciation. She later confessed that no one had ever done that for them. She said I would never know how much it meant to her family, but she was wrong. I did know. I was new to the neighborhood once, too.

In one Asian country the people greet each other not with, "How are you?" but with, "Have you eaten rice today?" If the reply is affirmative, then the assumption is that all the needs of the people are satisfied. An old saying advises that a bird in the hand is worth two in the bush. If that bird is cooked, give it to a new neighbor and fun is assured for you both.

37

Present a slide show.

Many souvenirs from delightful past experiences are stored in boxes, in closets, and under beds. If some of those souvenirs happen to be photographic slides, find them, dust them off and throw a party! A slide show can be great entertainment for friends and a wonderful way for you to re-visit memories.

While we were on our honeymoon in Hawaii and California, Dickie and I brought the memories of that dream-come-true vacation home with us on slides.   We photographed mountains and oceans, waterfalls and streams. We captured orange, lemon, pineapple, coconut and banana trees . . . all laden with fruit. We snapped shots of birds perching on poles, chipmunks eating from our hands and goldfish swimming under Japanese bridges. Perhaps the most beautiful slides were of the sunsets. Hardly a moment of our honeymoon went undocumented.

Within a week of our return home, we watched our slide show. The viewing took two hours. Then we put the screen and slides away for what turned out to be months but could have been years had it not been for our friend Tom.

Tom went to Hawaii and took slides too. While he was telling us about his experiences, we decided to share our slides with friends. We planned a party with a Hawaiian theme. Out of kindness for our guests, Tom and Dickie selected only the best of our slides for the show. Maybe our friends were just being nice; but, when the evening was over, they unanimously admitted they had a good time.

With friends and family members alike, slides create an excuse for a party. And with slides, unlike pictures, you can show them to many people at one time. Slides expose fun in each frame. Process some for yourself!

38

Send funny greeting cards.

Do you have a friend or loved one who is in the hospital? Mail him a laugh! Laughter is, after all, the best medicine. Do you know someone who is unemployed? Mail her a laugh. She's already depressed, so don't add to the feeling with somber words.

When someone gets married, how many funny cards do you think they receive? Be different! Send a funny greeting. Let's face it. Marriage is hard work. If the couple can't laugh together, the union is on rocky ground from the beginning.

My friend Opal Worthy was a saint, well into her nineties, possessing a keen sense of humor. With friends in high and low places, scattered around the world, she received dozens of greeting cards each month. I was surprised when I sat by her bed one day and heard her exclaim, "At last! A funny greeting card!" She could tell I didn't understand, so she explained. "People keep expecting me to die soon, so they send me cards with prayers on them and pictures of heavenly skies. I may be in my nineties, but I don't plan to die anytime soon. And even if I do, I'm alive today, and I want to enjoy it to the fullest!"

Funny cards don't mean that you are insensitive to the hurts of others. Your kind, hand-written comments inside the card reflect your concern. Funny cards do imply that

 sunshine will follow the rain and joy will be found in the morning. Be a good friend by sending your friend a reason to laugh.

39

Form a support group.

Though opportunities for fun are always within your reach, circumstances sometimes prevent you from seeing them. During these times you need help finding your joy. Form a support group. Invite friends to meet with you on a regular basis and make laughter and positive thinking your goals.

I remember a period in my teaching career that was so chaotic, I almost lost sight of my love! That year the Education Reform Act of 1982 was passed, standardizing course content and holding teachers accountable for student achievement. The paper work, logistics and compromises involved were outrageous.

Meanwhile, I still had a debate team to coach, a play to direct, a show choir to choreograph and classes to instruct.

The students felt the tension, and everyone was on edge. One thing was for sure—I wasn't having fun anymore.

While praying about the situation one morning, I thought about all the fun-loving teachers who enjoyed teaching as much as I did. Surely they, too, longed for the "good old days," when we laughed in the hallways and classrooms. I went to each one with a plan to form a teacher support group. The group would be composed only of positive people who love what they do. Everyone agreed and we decided to meet once a month. The only requirement was that if we talked about school, the content had to enumerate the good things that were taking place in our classrooms.

This fellowship became a tremendous boost. Sharing positive ideas helped to keep us focused on the main reasons we were teachers—to teach and to develop in young people a love for learning.

Good, therapeutic support groups already exist for many emotionally and physically challenged people. If you want to give your sense of humor some therapy, form a support group of fun-loving people. Two heads for laughter are definitely better than one.

40

Capture fun on video tape.

Put your video camera to use for more than just special occasions. Any rainy day will do; or even a sunny afternoon when Susie announces, "I'm bored." Put it to use at parties. Make a family reunion memorable. Re-enact your history. Preserve your collective knowledge for future generations.

My somewhat limited skills using a video camera saved the day one summer during Vacation Bible School. Vacation Bible School is a weeklong event sponsored by churches of various denominations. Generally, young people, five years old and up, come to the church for a full morning of Bible study, arts and crafts, music, games and refreshments. Like many teachers who have summers free, I often volunteered to help with this week of summer fun.

This particular summer I was assigned to teach 15 fifth-graders. As luck would have it, only two of the three workers planned for the group showed up. With our best energetic theatrics, we told stories, carved wood and sang songs, nonetheless, the children became restless. We needed heavier artillery. The "big gun" we turned to for help was a video camera.

The next morning, instead of just telling the Bible stories, we re-enacted them. We hastily gathered makeshift props and costumes. We rehearsed staging and dialogue only once, and then the film rolled. As soon as the project was finished, we scrambled to a television and watched our masterpiece. Though not Hollywood quality, we were proud of what we did.

On commencement night, when the parents came to see the students' work, we had no arts and crafts to display. We could, however, recite Bible verses, sing songs and re-enact scenes. Each student took home their own copy of the video tape.

Video cameras are like knives that cut through the mundane and offer us two edges of social fun: 1) the fun of taping, and 2) the fun of watching.

41

Share a snack.

Snacks sustain you from one meal to the next, give your energy levels a boost and serve as great social icebreakers. Offer your guests candy sweethearts in July, long after Valentine's Day has passed. Substitute chow mein noodles for crackers when you serve grapes and juice. Keep some cashews handy and munch occasionally on marshmallows.

One day I was sitting in an airport lobby waiting for a delayed plane, joined by a hundred or so other people. The air was stuffy, and customer patience was wearing thin. I was struck by the fact that, of these 100 or so people, no one seemed to be talking.

Beside me sat a family including two small children. I watched as the father, and then the mother, and then the father, etc., tried to entertain them. The children were losing it, and so were the parents.

From my carry-on, I removed a sack of multi-colored, flavored jellybeans. I rattled the sack and instantly drew the children's attention. Catching the mom's eye for approval, I pulled out one of the candies and said to the children, "You can have this one, if you can tell me what color it is." They looked at their mom, who nodded her approval, and the oldest one yelled, "It's yellow!"

We guessed colors and flavors, numbers and names for the next 30 minutes. Miraculously, the plane arrived and the game ended. The mom and dad thanked me profusely for helping entertain the children, admitting they were weary of the challenge. I took the thanks, but I knew that the jellybeans deserved the applause. What a great snack!

Fun-filled snacks are limited only by your imagination. Be sure to invite someone to share them with you.

42

Start a supper club.

The scene is universal. We see friends at church, or in the mall, and agree that we must get together soon. One will say, "Call me," as we start in opposite directions. The other will yell, "You call me." As the distance becomes greater, you faintly hear both saying, "I will." With the passage of years, getting together with friends seems to become harder, not easier. Schedule time together. Start a supper club!

When Dickie and I first married, we had a group of friends with whom we spent much time. However, as time passed and our lives changed, getting our group of seven assembled in one place became virtually impossible. We missed each other and talked about starting a supper club, but nothing happened.

One year for Dickie's birthday, I proposed to these friends that we throw him a surprise party and they agreed. To keep Dickie from suspecting anything, each family agreed to bring a food dish. After all, no one has to take a vegetable to his own birthday party. SURPRISE!

Even more surprising was how easy the party was to plan when everybody brought a part of the meal. At last, the phantom supper club had begun! With four houses represented, we agreed to rotate the location each month. The host would be responsible for the meat dish and for telling the rest of us the type of food to bring.

Once we started meeting, we spent the first two months trying to decide on a name for our club. The Grub Club was my favorite suggestion, but the idea lacked sophistication for the rest of the group. We finally decided on THE STERLING SEVEN.

At some dinners we actually use the sterling silver service, though stainless and plastic flatware have been called into service, too. Sterling or stainless, the fun is sensational. I highly recommend that you start a supper club with friends of your own.

43

Picnic.

Laughter is one of the most successful ways of bonding a group of people together. Games make team players of us all, teach cooperation and generate goodwill and laughter. Playful events don't occur without planning; so, set aside a day periodically for games and picnics.

"Dickie, where are you going dressed like that?"

"To work."

"In running shorts and a T-shirt?"

"Sure. The base is having a picnic today, and a 5K race is kicking it off first thing this morning."

Keesler Air Force Base holds an annual picnic for employees. Offices are staffed with minimal personnel, the dress of the day is casual, and playful games reign supreme. By staying on the grounds, but setting the work aside for a day, soldiers and staff can remember why they work so hard at our nation's defense—to protect our life, liberty, and pursuit of happiness.

On one occasion, Dickie and I were returning home from a weekend outing with food still left in the ice chest. Rather than grab a hamburger for lunch, we drove out of our way to a state park with a lake. We spread our lunch on a picnic table and began to relax. The spot was shady, cool, and quiet. The scenery was picturesque. The leftover potato salad and cold fried chicken actually tasted good. After eating, we walked by the water's edge and climbed on nearby rocks.

"All work and no play" has long been the directions to Dullsville. Given the busy schedules of most people, it's not wise to expect games and picnics to just happen. Deliberately set aside a day to play.

44

Say "Hello."

Greeting people is such a friendly thing to do; and, if you do it right, the greeting can mean fun for everyone. Ed Foreman is a motivational speaker who encourages people to answer the standard question, "How are you?" with the energetic reply, "Terrific!" He contends that if we will deliberately choose a cheerful greeting, we can trick the subconscious into believing what we say. As a result, the subconscious will go to work to produce that wonderful feeling.

Biblical teaching actually supports this thought. Matthew 12:34b (KJV) states, "For out of the abundance of the heart the mouth speaketh." Proverbs 23:7 (KJV) tells us, "For as a man thinketh in his heart, so is he." If we speak what we think, and what we think is what we are, reason dictates that we should think and speak positive words.

People who grow up in the South are taught to speak to

total strangers. "Hello." "Good afternoon." "Hi, there." "How are you?" No one expects to engage in conversation. We are just taught that greeting people is polite. You'll understand, then, why I was surprised in New York City.

I was walking with a friend down the crowded streets, straining my neck to see the tops of buildings. As I passed people and caught their eyes, I chirped out a cheery hello. After only a few greetings, my friend asked me to please refrain. He feared we would be mugged. New York was his town, not mine, so I didn't question his wisdom, but I did grieve for the loss.

"Hello!" is such a small gift and requires so little of us. We live in a big, wide world. Make the world more wonderful by greeting people cheerfully.

45

Hoop it up on holidays.

Hoop is the shortened form of the word hoopla, which means excited commotion.

Need a reason to hoop it up? Just look at the calendar. The year is peppered with holidays like New Year's Day, Martin Luther King, Jr. Day, Groundhog Day, Valentine's Day and Presidents Day, just to name a few. Even if you're not Irish, you can celebrate in honor of St. Patrick's Day. Be sure to wear green and pinch those who don't. Round out the year with a few religious holidays like Christmas, Easter, Yom Kippur and Hanukkah and the result is a yearly cup filled to the brim with food, fun and fellowship.

The fourth of July is a fantastic holiday for kicking back and having a good time. All you need is a day off work, food, decorations, games and a healthy supply of family and friends.

Dickie loves to grill outdoors on this patriotic day. Party guests bring green salad, potato salad, baked beans, buns, chips and dip. We supply the hamburgers, condiments and soft drinks. We hang flags around the gazebo, place cushions in the outdoor chairs, and place colorful cloths over the folding tables. As people begin to arrive, smoke and the smell of cooking burgers permeate the air. The party has begun.

Great parties rarely "just happen." Volunteer your house or commandeer a friend's home. Get on the telephone and find at least six people who will agree to come. Just make sure you keep it simple and plan for fun.

You can't expect humor to always come naturally. Often the stage must be set for its arrival. Holidays provide the ideal platform from which to spring into a fun-filled time. Hoop it up! A refreshing splash of humor awaits you.

46

Join a community theater.

In the play *As You Like It*, William Shakespeare wrote "All the world's a stage, and all the men and women merely players." If sometimes you would like to play a part other than the one you play each day in life, join a community theater. Fun and excitement are waiting for you at the stage door.

When I was 23 years old, just out of college and working at my first job, I received an invitation to audition for the leading role in Gulfport Little Theater's summer musical, *The Man of La Mancha*. That invitation turned into a lifelong courtship with Little Theaters.

On the night of the tryouts, dozens of people auditioned for the musical. Even though acting parts weren't available for everyone, dozens of opportunities awaited backstage.

A place of service existed for every would-be participant. Over 100 people were actually involved in the production. The list included actors, musicians, stagehands, set builders, artists, seamstresses, publicity committees, ticket promoters, program designers, plus lighting and sound crews. Community theaters are a gold mine for potential friendships and fun.

When *The Man of La Mancha* ended, I remained active in the theater, participating in every aspect, including serving on the Board of Directors. I went from knowing a handful of people in Gulfport to knowing hundreds of people in a matter of weeks. Over the years, many of those people have become dear friends.

If your schedule prohibits the addition of one more time-consuming activity, attending plays at community theaters can still be a great source of social fun. Most Little Theaters mount five shows during a season, each offering a great night of entertainment.

Community theaters unite people and develop their skills. The art form brings an element of culture to a city that heightens the cities humanity. And, if you should ever have the time, a place of service will be waiting there for you!

47

Telephone a friend.

Have you got a good recipe? Did you hear a new joke? Can you recommend a funny movie? Pick up the phone and share it with a friend. Practice short conversations. Rotate through a list of friends with whom you want to keep in contact. To elevate your fun quotient socially, add joyful telephone calls to your daily routine.

My niece was born in southern California while my parents and I sat waiting for the news in south Mississippi. When the telephone finally rang, great shouting and cheering erupted. "It's a girl!" The announcement was fun and enjoyed by all.

Years later, our mother lived with me in Mississippi while my brother J. lived in California. Since Mom was weak and couldn't place the calls to J. herself, my brother and I began calling each other every week or so, talking about projects, vacations, friends, plans, politics, religion, you name it. Jokes crept into our conversations as we shared the latest ones we had heard. Mom enjoyed listening to our chatter on an extension and chiming in when she felt well enough. J. and I are both grateful for the time we spent chatting long distance for Mom's sake.

Computer email is more economical than the telephone in time and money in some respects, but nothing substitutes for the familiar sound of a friendly voice on the other end of a line. Either way, put communication technology to work . . . for the fun of it!

SECTION III

MENTAL FUN

48

Mentally clock-out.

Make it a practice to physically and mentally leave the office at the end of the day. Arriving home, shift gears by doing something totally unrelated to your job. Play ball with a youngster, visit friends, work on a hobby or read a good book.

My husband was employed with a state agency when I first met him. He enjoyed his job but rarely brought work home, and he never talked about it. Often people asked, "What do you do at the agency, Dickie?" He responded, "I'm a typical bureaucrat. I push a lot of paper." No further explanation was ever given.

Many people let employment consume their waking thoughts. They glamorize this as being devoted to their professions. However, perhaps they're just poor managers of their time or they accept too many responsibilities. For whatever reason, most people have far too many tasks to complete in a full workday. So they cart paperwork home; make endless phone calls at night; fret, plot, and plan for the next day, week, month, even years!

I am an advocate for excellence in work. Mediocrity can destroy you; but don't lose sight of a balanced life. Humans are physical, mental, emotional, social and spiritual creatures. Time must be given to develop all five of these areas if you are to be healthy. Your career must not become totally life consuming.

Plan time for fun and relaxation each evening, just as you plan for work. Tomorrow is another day.

49

Start a fun diary.

Nothing crystallizes a thought like writing it down. Writing activates the body and the mind. The thought is made visual. We remember it better. Start a fun diary. The diary will serve to remind you of the good times. You can refresh your spirit by remembering that life has been, and still is, filled with goodness.

I required my students to attend theatrical productions on our campus. Prior to the first performance, I lectured on proper audience behavior. In the lecture, I berated the use of beepers and cell phones during the play.

On one particular opening night, one of my students was sitting next to a patron whose beeper sounded during Act I. As I approached the patron at intermission to request that the beeper be left with the house manager, I overheard my student warning her, "Beware, the beeper patrol will get you." When my student saw me, she was embarrassed, but we both laughed. I've been called many things, but that was a first—Beeper Patrol!

Later, when I tried to tell a colleague what the student said, I struggled to remember. I then ran and jotted it down. "The Beeper Patrol" is now in my fun diary.

Humor happens everywhere—offices, homes, hospitals and parks. Jot the event's punchline down on anything handy. Arriving home, scribble it into a diary. Months or years from now, the diary will remind you that life, though filled with difficulties and disappointments, is still worth living. Read, remember, laugh and renew.

50

Speak in a foreign language.

Speak in a foreign language to add variety and humor to your life. The more proficient you are with a language, the more fun you can have. You might even want to learn a whole new language. Mastering the language is mentally stimulating, providing a wealth of material for your humor efforts. If you don't seem to have the time and inclination to learn a whole language, then memorize some choice words, phrases, quotations or songs.

In Terrence McNally's play, *Lip's Together, Teeth Apart,* the character Chloe occasionally slips French phrases into her conversations, beginning a line in English and ending it in French. After several utterances of Chloe's foreign penchant, the character Sally asks her why she does this. Chloe responds, "Because I've grown bored with English."

My junior high history teacher was versed in Latin. Our class often made a game out of guessing what the phrases meant. Ex Post Facto was translated, in jest, as, "Exit this place, Fatso." E Pluribus Unum might bravely become "I have two bus tickets to Unum." History was never the same for me after that class.

We enjoy foreign languages because we respond to the unexpected. Unique tones awaken us. For example, music that follows the same cadences and chord progressions is predictable and can be uninspiring. However, music that syncopates an unexpected note and modulates into a different key is thrilling. The same is true of speech. So, take advantage of our natural desire to enjoy "the different." Much fun can be had with adios, au revoir, atachitory-catchetory-later!

51

Pretend!

Given the right time, place and company, pretending is refreshing. We all must play expected roles. The judge must be serious. The teacher must maintain control. The salesman must be credible. Pretending frees us from the expected.

"Oh, Wellington, bring me my car. And Beulah, fetch my bag." I laugh when I hear him sound the familiar phrases. You see, my friend Andy pretends to be a wealthy aristocrat with a chauffeur and cook. The pretense usually comes when we're making light of the fact that we can't do something for lack of money.

One night we dressed in formal attire and dined in the nicest restaurant in town, acting the sophisticated charade throughout dinner. With heavy English brogues, we told the waiter about our game and asked him to play long, just for fun. And it was fun.

Parents have long pretended to be horses for children to ride atop. Big brothers have been Earth Station Zebra calling Planet Mars. Little girls have cut out paper dolls and given them voices and characters.

Pretending is not weird. Imagination happens naturally. For the sake of fun, I recommend pretending more often.

52

Read amusing books.

Read something funny. Become full of joy and wit. Sit in a comfortable chair, sip on your favorite beverage and get lost in the lines of a fascinating book. It's great entertainment.

Sir Francis Bacon said, "Reading maketh a full man." Henry David Thoreau wrote in his book *Walden,* "Books are the treasured wealth of the world and the fit inheritance of generations and nations . . . How many a man has dated a new era in his life from the reading of a book!"

Most people are not speed-readers. Sometimes finishing a book takes me weeks, reading only one chapter each night before I fall asleep. I have yet to find a book I can't put down, no matter how good it is. But, the few lines I read before sleep overtakes me serve as medicine to my mind and spirit. They refresh me. Positive reading material equips me to see the good in people, the joy in living. I laugh at others' mistakes. The courage of the character, the wisdom of the author and the beauty of the description inspire me.

Sages throughout the ages have advised the wise man to read. I say if you're going to read, read something funny. Everyone has a sense of humor, but not everybody finds the same things funny. Experiment with your humor. Discover what you think is funny, then read, read, read. Don't delay. Find a book that gets you started toward adding more humor to your life.

53

Visualize.

Visualize any reoccurring setting at home or work. In that setting, see yourself using a humor suggestion: telling a joke at the staff meeting, leading students in songs, distributing smiley faces at hospitals . . . anything! Repeat this scenario in your mind as often as time allows. Notice exactly what you are doing and resolve to perform the activity that way in reality.

A high school football player, intensely recruited by colleges as a field goal kicker, explained that while he was at school, home, church or wherever, he imagined himself on the football field, kicking toward the goal. He saw where he was standing, where the ball was placed and how many steps were required to kick it. He saw himself kicking the ball, following through with his body and watching the ball go through the goal posts.

Daily he practiced this mental game, placing the ball all over the field. When the time came to kick the ball in the actual game, he settled himself down by recalling his mind pictures, and he behaved like he saw himself performing. His success rate was proof that it worked.

You may be thinking, "I'd like to use these ideas for adding humor to my life, but I could never tell a joke, let alone lead a song!" Don't let shyness, fear or uncertainty keep you from enjoying any of these fun-loving suggestions. Use visualization techniques. Seeing is believing, and believing empowers action. If you just try, fun can be your companion for a lifetime. Can you see it yet?

54

Divide and conquer.

Choose any goal: writing a book, buying a new house, cleaning out the garage, jogging in a 10K race, refinishing furniture or graduating from college. Focus on your goal. Now brainstorm. Look for ways to break this huge goal into small tasks that can be accomplished in 15-minute time periods. Commit to work on your goal for that short amount of time as often as possible. Then reward yourself regularly as you work toward the goal.

One of my long-term goals was to vacation in Italy. My first step toward getting there was to brainstorm and determine the many small tasks that had to be accomplished before this long-term goal could be realized. First on my list was the need to get Dickie to agree with me, which took several 15-minute time blocks.

Once in agreement, we bought travelers' guides and

seized every minute possible to read and discover Italy's different cities, historical sites, hotels and restaurants. Other tasks on the list included

things like developing a savings plan, scanning an encyclopedia to learn the history, checking on airline tickets and money exchanges, learning common Italian phrases and studying schedules to determine the best time to travel.

When the list of needed tasks was made, Italy was still a long time away, but our fun was immediate. We rewarded ourselves as we went with hugs and kisses, ice cream, and dinners out. We finally accomplished our goal of travelling to Italy. Believe me, it was worth the effort!

To ensure that your "good things" get done, plant seeds of fun in your garden of goals.

55

Prepare humorous responses.

Do you deal with complaining customers, sick patients, fussy children or angry citizens all day? Rather than letting them eat away at your nerves, be proactive. Instead of giving the standard song and dance routine, why not plan a delightful response? The time and effort required to create a humorous answer for a reoccurring problem is well invested.

Students in my speech classes panicked on the day of their first graded presentation. Some became nauseated. Other students trembled, hardly able to stand and deliver the speech. To relax them, I told a couple of jokes about famous speakers who were nervous. The students laughed, and the fear lost some of its grip. I then took the classroom trashcan and held it up, pointing out its location, and that it was fully lined with a leak-proof bag, should anyone need it while speaking. I told them we would wait patiently until they finished regurgitating, and then they could proceed with the speech . . . no points deducted. Predictable laughter followed this explanation, and no one ever used the trashcan.

Think about a problem you face regularly. Has something funny ever happened while you were dealing with that problem? Can you share that story with the new people involved in the problem? Can you make and post on the wall a cartoon about the situation? Humor really is a medicine that can heal wounded spirits—yours and the customer's.

56

Increase your vocabulary.

Learn as many new words as possible. In addition to helping you understand humor, new words strengthen and enrich your vocabulary.

A businessman was dissatisfied with the never-ending paper shuffle in his office; so he resigned and marched to the Port of Houston to apply for work. The personnel office gave him a job unloading cargo ships. His first shipment included blacksmith anvils. Eager to work by the sweat of his brow, even with the forklift broken, he rolled up his sleeves and began carrying the anvils from the ship across the plank to the dock. On one of the trips across, the plank broke! He fell into the water and went under the first time. Then, he went under a second time. And just before he went under the third time, he yelled, "If someone doesn't help me, I'm going to drop one of these anvils!"

This joke predictably results in a hearty laugh when told to older audiences. However, when I told it to a high school audience, the punch line reaped only polite chuckles. Curious, I paused in my presentation and asked the students why. The students' response was, "What is an anvil?"

Don't make a habit of simply ignoring or skimming over words that you don't understand. Instead, jot them down, look them up in the dictionary and repeat the definitions until you have them memorized.

Learning one word may take several days. Take out your dictionary and pick an "A" word today, a "B" word next week, and so on. Make a game out of trying to use the new word in conversation during the day. Share the word with co-workers. If you don't know the definition, they probably don't either.

If you are not already familiar with the word "cachinnate," consider starting your fun with it. "Cachinnate" means to laugh loudly. Sounds like a great idea to me. I plan to cachinnate often today. I hope you will, too.

57

Mix sugar with your medicine.

A negative attitude about performing an everyday responsibility often causes stress. Perhaps the task at hand is difficult, requiring more energy than you want to give. Perhaps you dislike the assigned detail because you don't know how to do it, nor care to learn. Maybe you think someone else should be doing it instead of you. Zig Ziglar, author of *See You at the Top,* calls these attitudes "stinkin' thinkin'."

Conceivably, you may be relieved of a responsibility by fussing and complaining, but that doesn't build self-esteem or gain the respect of others. When saddled with an unpopular task, be creative. Any job can be transformed into fun with a little imagination.

I knew a delightful lady who hated to vacuum. The

upright vacuum cleaner was heavy. Maneuvering under and around furniture was exhausting. Furthermore, no one ever seemed to notice whether she vacuumed or not! So, to make that task more pleasant, she played her favorite country music loudly on the stereo and did the Texas Two-Step across her floors. She was no longer vacuuming. She was dancing, and she loved to dance!

I don't like to do dishes, so I made a game out of stacking dishes in the dishwasher. I have actually unloaded the dishwasher and started over again just to get that one last glass in the top shelf. Who cares that it took more time? I played a game with my dishes, and I won.

The lyrics from a *Mary Poppins'* tune advise, "Just a spoonful of sugar helps the medicine go down in a most delightful way." Take your medicine, whatever the task may be, with a positive attitude. Do the unpleasant task, but be creative throughout the entire process. Sugar comes in many forms! Measure it liberally.

58

Recite poetry!

Memorize and recite fun poetry. You can do it. It's easy!
Choose a poem you like and learn only a few lines at first.
Next, review the lines and add a few more, continuing until
you've memorized the entire poem.

Immediately start reciting the poem you've memorized
at every opportunity. The words will eventually move from
the surface level of knowledge into the deeper, more perma-
nent region of the brain. Then, when you need an attention
device for a speech or a clever comment in conversation, the
poem will delight your listeners.

My students always laughed when I recited this little
ditty recorded by Louis Armstrong—sometimes I sang it!

> *I'll take the legs from some old table*
> *I'll take the arms from some old chair*

I'll take the neck from some old bottle
And from a horse I'll take the hair

I'll take the hands and face from some old clock
And baby when I'm through
I'll get more loving from the dum-dum-dummy
Than I ever got from you

Remember, a word "fitly spoken" is powerful and the power turns to pleasure when the words are humorous. Among my favorite poems are the limericks of Ogden Nash:

A jolly young fellow from Yuma
Told an elephant joke to a puma;
Now his skeleton lies
Beneath hot western skies—
The puma had no sense of huma.

An added advantage to memorizing poetry is that you are using your brain. You must never stop learning new information. Like any other organ or muscle, use it, or lose it. Hey! That's poetic! Choose to use it.

59

Sleep on it.

Our last thoughts prior to falling asleep are replayed in our subconscious minds throughout the night. Therefore, let your last thoughts before sleeping work to relieve stress and restore energy. Instead of reading newspapers late at night or watching the evening news, select funny reading material or watch programs that make you laugh. Avoid negative thoughts as you near bedtime.

If you enjoy being fully informed, or if your job requires that you stay abreast of current events, gain the information during the day. After all, little can be done about a volcano in Peru or corruption in Washington after 8 p.m. anyway.

In addition to helping us get a good night's sleep, positive thoughts prior to sleep can actually be useful in solving problems. Author John Steinbeck states, "It is a common experience that a problem difficult at night is resolved in the morning after the committee of sleep has worked on it."

If you have a problem you can't seem to solve, as you are falling asleep, imagine the problem working out the way you wish it to in reality. While you are sleeping, your subconscious mind will continue to work on the problem, identifying thoughts overlooked by the conscious mind and mapping out a route to the desired outcome. You will begin to make decisions based on promptings from your subconscious mind, resulting in the desired solution.

When I first wrote fun suggestion #74, titled "Work to music," I couldn't think of a good parallel example to explain the importance of the suggestion. That night before sleep, I prayed, asked God to help me, and imagined myself waking in the morning with the perfect idea. While I was getting dressed the next morning, I thought of the painting "Mona Lisa." When you read #74, see if you agree that it is a good comparative example.

Tonight, when you go to bed, think positive thoughts. Sweet dreams!

60

Repeat joyful affirmations.

Proclaim good things about yourself, your work, your future and the people around you, and you will create and perpetuate an atmosphere where good things and good attitudes exist. Affirmations work! They become self-fulfilling prophecies. It's a fact. We tend to become what we talk about. If we constantly tell people how busy and overworked we are, we will only perpetuate the presence of the things that seem to keep us busy.

One school year I had a particularly rowdy and unmotivated class. Grades were terrible. Assignments were either not attempted, or when attempted, half done. Teacher frustration was high. I told everyone who would listen about this hour of torture I endured. Finally, as a test of the affirmation theory, I started telling other people, the students and myself that these difficult students were wonderfully talented young people. I mentally assigned each of them leading roles in my future; i.e. President of the United States, chief physician in a hospital, owner of a nursing home. Remarkable changes occurred. I grew to truly like these students, laughing with them more often. Class work and student interaction improved. The class became one of my favorites.

If you think this seems reminiscent of the children's story, *The Little Engine That Could*, you're right. In the story, the train climbed up the steep hill because the little engine kept saying, "I think I can. I think I can." Even the Bible teaches the wisdom of affirmations: "As a man thinketh in his heart, so is he." (Proverbs 23:7, KJV).

What terrible, uncomfortable, difficult, threatening, boring, painful, stupid thing do you have to endure? Try thinking and reciting out loud positive things about it. Start with phrases like: "I feel victorious today." "I enjoy my work." "I am healthy and happy." "I get along well with people." "I am a nice person to be around. " "Today is a great day!" You'll be on top of your mountain before you know it!

61

Embrace technology.

Few things have changed in America as fast as technology. A shopper buys the state-of-the-art today, and tomorrow the purchase is obsolete. That fact, coupled with the fear that somehow we can't understand it, prevents many people from trying to use technological advances. Embrace change—stopping it is impossible.

Visitors to an old monastery perched high atop a jagged mountain cliff were lifted to the structure in a large straw basket drawn by a rope and pulley system. One day, halfway up the cliff, one of the visitors noticed the rope was frayed. He turned to the monk guiding them and asked, "How often do you change this rope?" The monk calmly replied, "When the old one breaks."

Many of us treat change like the monks treated the rope. We'll do something about adapting to it when we have to, and not before.

Working in the fine arts, I deal with abstracts. Technology is concrete. This dichotomy renders me technologically challenged. However, I have eagerly tackled new technology. I can film with a camcorder. I'm familiar with PowerPoint® and multimedia presentations. I can surf the net, change the time on a multi-functional wristwatch and utilize a Personal Information Assistant. As technology changes, this list of newfangled skills will surely grow.

If you can conquer the fear of technology, learning to use it and determining how to incorporate it into your life is much easier. The feeling of accomplishment that comes with the newly acquired skills will have you jumping for joy.

62

Read a magazine.

Read a magazine. Particularly small magazines with short articles that can be read in two to five minutes. If the magazine is also positive in nature . . . TA DA! . . . a mental lift!

Most people are constantly on the go. Several times during the day you may find yourself with five minutes on your hands waiting behind a desk for a customer, in the doctor's office for an appointment or at the schoolyard for the bell to ring. Keep a magazine in your purse, briefcase or car for such occasions. While you wait, don't impatiently blow a fuse. Read!

Two of my favorite small magazines are *Reader's Digest* and *Guidepost.* I love the jokes and word power features in *Reader's Digest. Guidepost* is full of stories about courageous people who embrace life and make the world a better place. The content from both sources is easy to read, fun and encouraging.

Many such magazines exist covering a wide variety of subjects. You'll find most are relatively inexpensive and require no membership or affiliation. When you are finished, pass your magazines on as great gestures of kindness to friends who need a boost. Important gifts do come in little packages, especially small magazines.

63

Make an appointment for fun.

Fun is a luxury we afford ourselves only if we have time. Since fun is so important, plan for it, just as you plan for meetings, rehearsals, haircuts and dentist appointments. Sit down with your calendar and make a conscious effort to schedule activities that will cause you to laugh out loud—boisterously. Plan something to enjoy today and something for the future. Always know that "laughter is on the way."

Merriam-Webster's Collegiate® Dictionary, 10th Edition, defines *enjoy* as "having for one's use, benefit; to take pleasure or satisfaction in." The word fun, however, is defined as "playful, often boisterous action or speech; it usually implies amusement and laughter." The health benefits, so touted in modern writings, come mainly from laughter, less from simple enjoyment.

The fun you schedule today might be to stop and get a snow cone on the way home from work or to have lunch with a friend you rarely see. The future's fun might be as close as tomorrow or as distant as next year. You can look forward to a weekend get-away, costume party or a major family vacation.

For one person, the fun might require physical action, like a rousing game of tennis or racquetball. For another, a funny movie or humorous book will do the trick. Whatever you plan, be as faithful to accomplish these activities as any on your list. While you may not receive money for them, you will receive life. Think about it. Which is more valuable?

64

Learn to play a musical instrument.

Learn to play an instrument—any instrument. The possibilities are endless. Perhaps you prefer a guitar, flute, harmonica or an accordion. There are so many delightful instruments to choose from.

My friend Don delights in playing a recorder—a simple version of the clarinet. Periodically, he shares a song with Dickie and me when we visit him for dinner. Another friend, Judy, plays the tambourine. Everything about the tambourine is fun—the size, the sound and the simplicity.

My instrument of choice is the piano. For years, my daddy sat in the living room, halfway reading his paper and halfway listening to me as I plunked through assigned pieces and chromatic scales. When I complained about my apparent lack of progress, Daddy usually replied, "Sounds like music to me." I often doubted the sincerity of that remark because on some days, Daddy would go to the far end of the house, shutting every door between us.

Learning to play an instrument requires repetition and can be a challenge to the player and those who are forced to listen. But after you learn, what a blessing a musical instrument can be!

I have walked into parties where conversation was still on the weather. Then, I would spy a piano, ask permission to play it and before long . . . voila! . . . a party was happening! People started singing and dancing. Talking grew louder as voices projected over the noise. Miraculously, a totally new atmosphere pervaded the room.

"Music soothes the savage beast." While learning to play the instrument may drive the beast crazy, mastering the instrument creates beauty and joy! Both learning and playing a musical instrument are sources of laughter.

65

Sign a humor contract.

Sign your name to a laughter contract to laugh out loud 10 times a day for a week. The contract does not need to be complicated. The wording might simply read: "I, Janie Walters, promise to laugh out loud 10 times each day for the week of June 8th–14th. Signed: _____."

Actually signing your name will make you feel more responsible. Make sure to list the days separately on the contract. The joy of accomplishment will reward you when you check each day off, affirming your laugher. If you get to the end of a day and find you are missing a few laughs, cram them in between brushing teeth and dressing for bed! The object is simply to laugh.

Many researchers who have studied humor conclude

that laughter produces numerous tangible benefits: reduces blood pressure, strengthens the heart muscle, boosts the immune system, controls stress, numbs pain and stimulates creativity.

With or without a mental stimulus, you can sit back and laugh your way to better health. While simply thinking a positive thought and smiling can result in some of these same benefits, the effects are far greater with the physical act of laughing.

So, write a contract. Sign it. Post the document where it can be seen. Have fun using that computer to make the contract look official. When 10 laughs a day are not enough, raise the number to 20, then 30. Beware! Laughter can be habit forming!

66

Think happy thoughts!

One positive thought is all it takes to turn your life around. So, if you want to reduce stress and add fun to your life, think a new, happy thought! Choose to think positive thoughts about your job, abilities, future and family. Empower your sentences with words like, "I can . . ." "I like . . ." "It's good . . ." If you must think of your past, choose to remember moments of laughter and success.

I remember a vacation once when Dickie and I walked through a pair of tall, iron gates and into a small, symmetrically landscaped garden. Much to my surprise, there he sat. As famous as he is, I expected him to be encased in glass. Nevertheless, I walked right up to him and stared. Rodin's "The Thinker" didn't seem to mind that I caught him naked. Rather, he continued to sit, carved in stone, posed in a position many of us rarely strike. He was just sitting in the French garden . . . thinking.

Norman Vincent Peale, a renowned minister and author of *The Power of Positive Thinking*, cautioned that people today stay on the go too much, allowing little time to sit and think. Peale reasoned that people expect good ideas to supernaturally come to them.

Indeed, ideas do "come to you" at times when you least expect them. Many of these random shots are brilliant and have tremendous impact. At other times, these spontaneous thoughts are dark, discouraging and fearful. Since the

thought gives birth to feelings and actions, you can't leave your thinking to chance. Happy thoughts produce happiness. Think about it.

67

Declare a "do-nothing" day.

A "do-nothing" day must be declared. It will never dawn by itself. Most people have a tendency to do something most of the time. Wherever we are, we see work that needs to be done. Though often too tired or lazy to do the work, we still think about it, doing mental work.

Try doing nothing for a whole day, or at least part of it. Responsibilities, when heaped on top of each other, become heavy burdens to bear. Learn to lighten up and reduce your own responsibility load. First read these sentences and then say them out loud: "I am not in charge of the universe. I have a right to just BE. The world will continue to spin without me."

My first successful "do-nothing" day came at the close of

one very busy school year. Rather than plunge immediately into a hectic summer schedule of traveling, cleaning, taking courses, and so on, I decided I had earned the right to do nothing for a day.

The night before my "do-nothing day," I went to the video store and rented six comedies. When the morning came, I assumed a prone position on the couch, watched consecutive movies, and laughed and sighed the day away, fixing only popcorn for lunch and ordering pizza for dinner. I was as relaxed as cooked spaghetti when the evening ended, and I arose the next morning refreshed and ready to start the summer.

The added benefit to doing nothing for a period of time comes when you actually learn how to enjoy just being . . . being still to watch an entire sunset, or swing in a hammock, or listen to children's chatter. To "work your way" into the joy of doing nothing, repeat frequently the

 following statement: "I am a human being, not a human doing."

SECTION IV

EMOTIONAL FUN

68

Laugh at yourself each morning.

Start every day with laughter. Should you need something to jump-start the laughter, just look in the mirror and laugh at yourself. For most of us, with hair askew and sheet marks plastered into our cheeks, we either have to laugh or cry, and laughter is healthier. Laughter stimulates the production of endorphins, the body's own natural form of morphine. You'll actually be anesthetized into feeling better. If you feel better, you'll look better.

I wear dramatic make-up. Each morning, I'm an artist. The make-up is my paint and my face is the canvas. First I apply subtle foundation, powder and daring blush. Then I decorate my eyes with bold colors of green, blue, purple or brown, depending on the outfit I have chosen for the day.

Soft black outlines my eyelids and highlights my lashes. I finish it off with vibrant raspberry colored lipstick. What a masterpiece! Some people might refer to my make-up efforts as "putting my best foot forward." Others might jeeringly call it "a charade." I call it self-defense!

F. Scott Fitzgerald, in his book *The Crack-up,* wrote, "The test of a first-rate intelligence is the ability to hold two opposed ideas in the mind at the same time, and still retain the ability to function." Even though you may feel like grunting when you look in the morning mirror, to demonstrate true intelligence, choose to laugh. These two opposing actions each possess colors with which to paint your face, thwarting or enhancing even the most expensive make-up. One action leaves a dull finish; the other leaves a shine. Laugh!

69

Clean out the clutter.

We lead cluttered lives. We cling to and store up unnecessary "things." At the time, these "things" probably seemed like a good idea. Maybe they were gifts. Perhaps the items were useful for a while but are no longer needed. Now, these "things" simply clutter our lives and our homes. Granted, cleaning an entire living space is a mammoth undertaking. However, if you take one drawer at a time, the task will be liberating and fun!

Kitchen drawers are a hoot to clean out, especially if you've been to as many Tupperware® parties as I have. My potato peeler occasionally gets lost in a sea of small, metal and plastic gadgets. I attack the drawer with determination to discard every unknown or never-used item. This project

always takes longer than anticipated because I discover neat doo-dads I forgot I owned!

During my last rampage through the kitchen drawer, I found a plastic tube with a large hole through one end. I deduced it was used to measure an individual portion of spaghetti. I'm not sure why I kept it. I never make a single portion of spaghetti. We cook in a big pot and eat spaghetti for days.

In the same drawer I uncovered a stainless steel pie server that looks like real sterling silver, a rubber-tipped gadget for picking up just one coffee filter at a time, a spoon used for steeping loose tea, and a casserole recipe I thought I'd loaned, never to see again. What a find! The plunder took about 10 minutes. I managed to part with four or five items, which reduced the clutter, and I smiled a lot in the process.

So, get started—one drawer at a time. Once you've cleaned out just one, the pressure is off. You've removed clutter from your life!

70

focus on the good.

When things are not going well at home, school, work, church or wherever you are, shift your focus toward the things that are going well. Make a list of all the negative things that could have happened, but didn't. Then throw a party to celebrate the things that are going right.

When I was a teacher, I had one class that was destined to be a challenge. This class was made up of the oddest assortment of college students imaginable. I remember walking into the room for the first time. My eyes scanned one young man reading a Bible and another one listening to a portable radio. Two students were wearing leather jackets with chains and others donned preppy pullovers and penny loafers. Mix all of these together in a course in which students are encouraged to express opinions and speak on subjects that interest them, and the chemistry can be dynamite.

By mid-semester, tension was high. One day, the students walked through the door arguing. I was struck with an inspired thought: Shift their thinking to the positive things they have in common.

In a cheerful, but determined tone, I announced my challenge. If the students, as a class, could come up with 100 positive things about the course and each other, I would cancel the next test and record A's for all of them. I was amazed at how quickly they embraced the challenge. Their list complimented every student, bragged about the class diversity and elevated me to sainthood! Miraculously, by shifting the focus from the negative to the positive, we created an entirely different chemistry. Most significant of all, everything about the class improved from that day forward . . . attitudes, behaviors and performances.

Choose to focus on the good in life, and then prepare to be delighted by all of the good you will see. Every cloud does have a silver lining. Find it, and then celebrate!

71

Develop a cartoon bulletin board.

One of the quickest and easiest sources of humor is a cartoon bulletin board. You can place your board anywhere. You can purchase inexpensive boards at a discount store or use a door facing in a pinch. The important thing is to have a central location where funny cartoons and slogans can be posted for easy access. Just find a place that you see daily, and you'll be in the humor business.

What should you post on your bulletin board? Use anything that makes you laugh. Comic strips are great sources of fun. Read them daily and post the ones that make you laugh. Don't overlook the potential in family photographs. Much of the clowning around that occurs during photo sessions produces contorted bodies and crazy facial expressions. Remembering the event adds to the fun.

I read a saying posted on a friend's bulletin board that I thought was funny, so I printed it and posted it on my own board. "EAT A LIVE TOAD FIRST THING IN THE MORNING AND NOTHING WORSE WILL HAPPEN TO YOU FOR THE REST OF THE DAY." Everyone who saw the sign for the first time would laugh, and I would laugh again, too.

A cartoon is like a little firecracker that carries a big bang. The spark it ignites in your heart may be all it takes to blast your emotions out of the doldrums and into delight. Go in search of something funny, and start your bulletin board today.

72

Whistle a happy tune.

Emotionally, whistling provides instrumentation for the song in your heart, and you don't even have to know the words. Make up a melody, and no one will be the wiser.

One of my mother's favorite reprimands to me was, "Janie, you need to change your tune." I usually wasn't singing at the time, but I knew exactly what she meant. She didn't like my attitude. Through the years, I've discovered that a good "attitude adjuster" is whistling. For those who can't whistle, substitute humming. The results are the same.

My dad taught me to whistle when I was a child. "Just pucker your lips, put your tongue behind your bottom teeth, and blow," he said. I followed those instructions for weeks before I ever produced anything but air. Then one day it happened. A real, musical note came out of my mouth! I couldn't wait for Daddy to get home and hear it. I was a child with a new toy. I whistled wherever I went.

Whistling has endless possibilities. I received a part in a play because I could whistle. My dog's ears perk up when I whip out a couple of sharp bursts. Whistling gets people's attention in crowds.

Whistle happy thoughts, regardless of the tune, and produce happiness. Come on! Pucker up and blow! Fill the air with the sound of joy.

73

Add color to ordinary things.

Bright colors cheer us, while dark colors depress us. Blue is calming; orange is exhilarating; red is passionate; and pink is romantic. Add color and pizzazz to ordinary, everyday things.

File folders are a perfect example. If you must look at beige, boring folders everyday, decorate them. Glue pictures of tropical island paradises or handsome, active people on the front covers. Scribble jokes on them, or label the folders with wacky names. Write in bright colored ink.

When I was nine years old, I scrounged some make-up from my mother's purse and applied it to my face. When I walked through the kitchen, Mother noticed my bright pink cheeks and cherry red lips and said, "Who gave you permission to use my make-up?" Then she launched into a long explanation of the phrase "pretty is as pretty does."

My dad overheard the conversation and came to my rescue, as he frequently did. He inserted, "Edna, make-up is not so bad. Any old barn looks better with a coat of red paint on it." I washed my face, but I never forgot that wise expression.

Bright colors paint the face of joy onto people and things. Decorate life with color. Stick a flower in a doll's hand; perch a cherub on a candle; hang a stained glass picture in the window. Tie a yellow ribbon around your own oak tree and welcome yourself home!!

74

Work to music.

The rhythms of background music toy with your emotions. If fun is your goal, choose up-tempo songs that allow you to sing along while you work, or military marches that match the energy and pace of your activity.

Picture Leonardo da Vinci's famous painting "Mona Lisa." Did the image of a plump young woman with dark hair and eyes, clear skin and a slight, intuitive smile come to mind? Unnoticed to the average viewer is a background filled with subtle, though magnificent scenery: a winding road leading to a river, bordered by trees, flanked by mountains, shrouded in a hazy, sunlit mist. Like this scenery, background music provides the focus for the foreground activity.

For background music to nurture humor and fun, choose your selection carefully. If the words of the song are about feeling blue or being broke, you will not feel joy. Melodies can also be counterproductive. Minor keys can trigger depression. Screeching high C's can be agitating. Repetitive phrases often become droning.

Frankly, I am not a morning person. Two alarm clocks are required to jolt my body from the sleeping dead. So what transforms me from a morning slug into a singing Pollyanna? The answer is music! As part of my morning routine, I listen to music. The positive lyrics and driving beat inspire my metamorphosis.

More than just a "get up in the morning" technique, cheerful music played in the background of any activity provides a platform from which joyful thought and action can spring. Do you want to have fun? Work to cheerful music!

75

Pamper your toes.

Pamper your toes with a massage or a soak in the tub. Come on! They deserve it. Most men's toes spend the entire day laced tightly in a hot shoe or smothered in a leather boot. Women's toes are squeezed together and forced into a tiny space called a high heel. After all that abuse, give your toes a break.

Not sure how to begin? Play a simple game to make it fun. You already know the rules. So, beginning with your big toe and moving toward your pinkie toe, say:

> *This little piggy went to market.*
> *This little piggy stayed home.*
> *This little piggy ate roast beef.*
> *This little piggy had none.*
> *And this little piggy cried "Wee, wee, wee"*
> *all the way home.*

Be sure to laugh when you get to the pinkie toe, even if you don't feel like it.

Get to know your toes by giving each one a name. As you rub each toe, make up a story about its life. Performing the toe massage in a nice warm bath heightens the experience.

I am aware that this particular suggestion sounds somewhat absurd. However, relieving our minds of the stress created by serious problems and physical exhaustion often requires absurd measures.

One night after a long day of being on my feet in a training session, I was stuck in an airport. Without even thinking about how it would look to other passengers, I slipped my foot out of my shoe, and massaged my toes. The rubdown felt so good, I eventually switched feet. I found myself squeezing my toes to the rhythm of a song I was humming. The big toe was the bass note. When the plane finally arrived, I placed happy feet back into my shoes and felt better all over.

The simple act of rubbing your toes can remind you to appreciate the dozens of small things on you and around you that are often taken for granted. A fantastic way to show appreciation is to squeal "wee wee wee" with joy!

76

Look for inside jokes.

Research indicates that of all the laughing that takes place during a day, only a small percentage occurs because of an actual joke. Most often we laugh at the funny things people do and say, the odd things we see and hear. When a group of people shares an experience that results in laughter, a friendly bond develops. The "joke" belongs to the group and establishes common ground.

Students in my public speaking classes were required to give persuasive speeches in which they attempt to sell items. In one class, John forgot to prepare the assignment. He was panicked, but not beyond thought. When I called on him, he jumped right up and began to sell us the only non-school item he had with him—a rechargeable electric razor. John's creative list of electric razor uses included: a baseball, a doorstop, a paperweight, a muscle massager and a pillbox hat, all of which he demonstrated with great flair.

When John's speech was over, he received a rousing round of laughter and applause from the class and from me. For the rest of the course, any time a student needed something they didn't have, someone would say, "Hey, John. Did you bring your razor?" The class would roar. If I misplaced my chalk or eraser, without looking up I would ask, "John, do you have your razor handy?" Predictably, laughter would follow. The class had formed a bond through this inside joke.

Do you need a laughter boost on your family vacation, in your office, with your staff or friends? Watch for inside jokes. The fun that results is worth any thought and effort the discovery requires.

77

Adopt a pet.

By definition, a pet is a "domesticated animal kept for pleasure rather than utility." (*Merriam-Webster's Collegiate® Dictionary*, 10th Edition) "Pleasure" only moderately explains the joy most people get from their pets. Laughter and frivolity, mixed with loyalty and love, compose the standard bill of fare. If you don't have a pet, I encourage you to adopt one.

Gucci, our dog, attracts attention wherever we go. His long, thin legs and tail, deep barrel chest, and high arched back are striking. A slender neck, long nose and erect, but flapped, ears, add the finishing touches to a regal animal. The first question people ask is usually, "What kind of dog is this?" We smile and say, "He's an Italian Greyhound, a smaller version of the large, racing Greyhounds. He was originally bred by the Italian aristocracy for the sole purpose of companionship, though some countries race them like the big Greys."

Before the unsuspecting inquirers can get a word in edgewise, they've been given the entire history of the breed and all of their characteristics. Finally, we launch into the stories about our life with Gucci, and we end by highly recommending the breed to anyone who wants a great pet!

How could one simple question set off that barrage of babble? The question triggered our favorite subject: our pet.

Being a responsible pet owner does require time and effort, but the investment in your fun quotient is worth it. Pets bring life and joy to a house. A pet is great company.

78

Brighten your world with candles.

Many of you have candles sitting on tables in your houses collecting dust. To add a sparkle of fun to your life, dust those candles off and light those wicks. The soft glow and soothing smell will make any room cozier. Not just for holidays, the flickering flame can inspire fun every day.

I prefer a vanilla-scented candle by my bedside. The smell calms me and readies my mind for sleep. A powder scent in the bathroom helps camouflage odors. With cinnamon in the living room and green apple in the kitchen, the family's appetite is guaranteed.

Our home is frequently the site of the annual Christmas dinner for the single adults of our church. Dickie and I decorate every corner and tabletop, making extensive use of candles. One party stands out in my memory, and I wasn't even there! When I returned home, I noticed that every candle in the house was burned down to the bottom, wax had dripped all over the holders and on the table, in some cases. Dickie explained that the electricity had gone off early during the party, and the candles provided the only light for several hours.

People who were at the dinner said things to me like, "This party was the best one yet!" "The power failure was a gift from God. We loved the candle atmosphere." "Sorry about your candles, Janie, but we sure had fun burning them." No apology was needed. The candles had given their lives for a noble cause—a party.

Candles are designed today to compliment every personality and interest. Colors exist for every décor. Masculine or feminine looking, with or without fragrances, the choice is yours. And if you're really creative, buy some paraffin and make your own.

Embrace the wide, wonderful world of candles. Set their wicks on fire and bask in the glow. Strike up some fun for yourself today. Light a candle.

79

Make a game of it.

Most days are filled with a plethora of boring, but necessary, tasks. Self-preservation demands that you make games of them. Can you hold your breath through the entire traffic light? Can you race your dog to the front door and win, or find 10 positive stories in the daily newspaper? Can you stuff one more piece of trash in the garbage can, or bring in all the bags from the grocery store at once? Challenge yourself, and the game commences.

Washing dishes offers a perfect example. No one really likes to wash dishes. I do it without complaining because it must be done. Electric dishwashers help tremendously; but, for those times when the washer is full, or the dishes are not safe in it, I wash dishes by hand. Here comes the fun! When the dishes in the sink out-number the size of the dish rack, I make a game of seeing just how many I can stack in the rack before one topples. Sometimes I rearrange the dishes in the rack to make room for just one more piece. Simply drying the dish would have been easier, but the game rules specify "in the rack."

A game to me is nothing more than an attitude of the heart. Games can be created from any activity as long as the heart is right. Not even recognized games are fun when attitudes are wrong. For example, tennis among friends becomes offensive when a racket is thrown at the net and card games cease to be fun when a player starts cheating. Fun is made, not by what we are doing, but by what we are thinking.

80

Listen to motivational tapes.

Knowing the importance of positive thinking, and thinking positively are two different things. The activities and emotions of a single day can be so negative that the mind has a difficult time just shifting out of reverse into neutral. The shift into drive, heading toward laughter, can seem impossible. Motivational tapes or CDs can provide the reinforcements you need.

To encourage me in my newly established speaking career, Mother bought me a set of motivational tapes called *Laugh Your Way to Success* by Rita Davenport. These tapes quickly became one of the most influential material gifts my mother ever gave me. I did laugh as I listened, but at the same time, I learned the importance of raising my expectations, establishing my confidence and self-esteem, managing my time, and developing enthusiasm.

From the *Laugh Your Way to Success* series, I went on to purchase tapes by noted motivators Zig Ziglar, Robert Schuller, Dwayne Dyer, Charles Swindoll and Ed Foreman. Each speaker, regardless of the specific subject addressed in the tape, repeatedly reminded me that I was a valuable person, loved by the Creator, responsible for how I felt, thought and acted. In different words, the same idea emerged from all the motivators: I may not always be able to choose my circumstances, but I can always choose my response to the circumstances.

So, when your schedule is loaded and you're feeling stressed, or your heart is breaking with sorrow, pop a motivational message into the nearest tape or CD player. Play the message loud enough to drive the garbage out of your brain and long enough to fill your mind with hope and joy. With these two champions behind the wheel of your thoughts, shifting into the high gear of laughter is a cinch!

81

Make a molehill.

"You're making a mountain out of a molehill." You know what it means: blowing things out of proportion, exaggerating, making a big deal over nothing. Knowing its meaning, however, and practicing its philosophy are worlds apart.

While problems do exist, more often than not you have allowed your imagination to build them into something bigger than they are. Instead, use your imagination to simplify problems rather than magnify them.

We are, at times, our own worst enemy. Occasionally, the papers I graded as an instructor overwhelmed me. During one insane semester, I had five assignments due within a two-week period from each of my 120 students. Grading became a mountain. I began climbing it by kicking myself. If I hadn't given so many assignments, papers would not pile up for me to grade!!

As with any major project, breaking the mountain of assignments into smaller stacks psychologically made a difference. I then had the foothills of a mountain. Each assignment rested in a different chair or on a different table-top. As I found small amounts of free time, I took one "foothill" and began to make a molehill, grading several papers at each sitting. Just devising a plan to complete the project made me feel better, and I seized the opportunity to applaud myself and laugh out loud. "Way to go, Janie! You're doing great!!"

Climbing mountains taxes all aspects of the body. You need strong arms and legs for hammering anchors into rocks, throwing ropes over ledges, swinging and pulling to the next location. You need a keen eye to determine the best angle to ascend, and a disciplined will to stay with the climb until you stand on the summit. Mountains in your life require the same exertion. Primarily, you must not forget to use your brain. THINK. Make a molehill!

82

Write a song.

If you have something to say, say it in the most creative way you can imagine—write a song! Songs don't have to rhyme or be lengthy or sound sophisticated. If the song is your creation, the words and melody will strike merry chords in your heart each time you sing it.

All through my teen years I loved writing poetry. I thought my poems were great. My reckoning day came during a poetry assignment in a college creative writing course. My poem contained an unexpected ending, and a style I had never used before. I was confident my natural talent would shine.

When the professor called on me, I distributed copies of my poem to the class and began to read. When I finished, the class was silent. I expected as much, after all, the surprise ending was designed to catch the audience off guard.

My professor broke the silence and said, "This poem is unacceptable college work. The contents belong on an eighth-grade bulletin board." Those words crushed me, and I never wrote poetry again.

Then one glorious Sunday at church, the minister enthusiastically preached from Philippians 4:13 (KJV), "I can do all things through Christ who strengthens me." Suddenly a whole song, complete with words and melody, popped into my head! As fast as I could, I wrote the words down.

If I think I can, I can,
Because I serve the great I Am,
Who said I can do all things through His pow'r,
If Christ I will receive.

There is nothing that's too great for me.
My dreams are free to wander,
For He said He'd always be with me,
If only I believe!

Israel's King David encouraged us to "Sing unto the Lord a new song." (Psalms 98:1, KJV) Why not write yours today?

83

Sip from crystal glasses.

Look around and find something you own that is beautiful and tangible. Most likely, you own something special that is put away for safekeeping. Why not take it out and use it? Crystal glasses work best for me.

Most young couples select a crystal pattern for their wedding. Each glass becomes a prize that sits protected in a china cabinet. At Christmas dinners, the crystal might grace the table, but great caution is used as the fragile stems are hand-washed and dried afterwards. This collected treasure is passed from mother to child to grandchild.

When I'm feeling "down in the dumps," I pull out my crystal and use it. The delicate, sparkling glass becomes a tangible weapon in the fight against self-pity. The beauty of the glass triggers positive thoughts, which can then soar and restore my optimism.

I feel special when I drink out of special glasses, even if the liquid is just water. While holding the glass in my hands, I'm more likely to recognize the many wonderful things I do have. When appreciation for life's little things returns, so will humor and joy.

84

Reminisce.

A Chinese proverb proclaims that one picture is worth more than a thousand words. One picture can also be worth a good laugh. Rummage through your photographs—new ones and old ones, those in albums and those still in developer's envelopes—and laugh as you go.

After years of storing family photos in a large cardboard box, my mother decided to sort through the pictures, organize them and place them in albums. Fourteen large albums later, the project was complete and today stands as a tribute to her incredible effort.

My baby pictures reveal that I started life as an adorable infant. By the time I reached 11 years old, I entered a homely stage, like I had fallen out of an ugly tree and hit every branch on my way down. The thought never occurred to me then that I wasn't beautiful; but now, I look at them and laugh. I call it my caterpillar stage, on my way to becoming a butterfly.

Along with my college graduation snapshots is a picture of my dad's truck piled precariously high with all my dormitory room contents. Furniture, boxes, posters, rugs and clothes were stacked on top of each other, supported only by rope and prayer. That picture reminds of all the funny and frustrating things we did and said trying to pack the truck so that one trip would suffice. I laugh again.

Our family albums enshrine pictures that date back to the 1800s. In that span of time, just imagine all the changes that have occurred in fashions, cars, houses, and careers. With weddings, birthdays, vacations, holidays, and baby pictures to browse through, the fun is guaranteed. Keep a camera handy. When you start to laugh, extend your arm and snap your own face. Talk about funny!

85

Celebrate Failure!

Though the adrenaline rush of success may leave your head spinning, the dizzying effects are rarely as crippling as the depressing effects of failure. Defeat is deadly and must be attacked with your strongest weapons. Humor to the rescue! Laughing at yourself is a good antidote for the feelings of failure. Laughter helps you acknowledge your weaknesses, forgive yourself for them, and celebrate the future prospects.

My niece Heather played on softball teams throughout her childhood, starting with T-ball. When school ended each year, a highlight in my summer was to go to California and see her play in person.

One of the first games I attended made a lasting impression on me. All the girls were very young and awkward. They threw the ball in every direction, rarely reaching the intended receiver. They swung the bat at every pitch. And when the girls ran, their caps flew off and their legs got tangled.

As luck would have it, the other team won. I feared Heather would be disappointed. After all, her Aunt Janie had flown in from Mississippi to watch her play. My lead comment was, "Sweetheart, I'm so sorry your team lost." Before I could go on and be clever, Heather asked, "Did we lose? What was the score?" I was startled. How could she not know the other team had 17 runs to her team's 3? My brother jumped in and saved me the embarrassment with, "Who cares what the score was? My little girl played a great game, and I'm proud of her. Let's go have pizza!"

Rudyard Kipling, in his poem "If," refers to winning and losing as "two impostors," one disguises itself as superior and belittles the other. Neither victory nor defeat represents the totality of what we are. Into every life both will come. Our goal is not to be ruled or rattled by either, but to learn from both. So just like we do with victories, celebrate failure. Throw a party. Order pizza.

86

Say "YES."

Say "YES" as often as possible to life, love and laughter.

Say yes to life. One summer, I was marooned on a couch for eight weeks following two major surgeries in seven days. The first week, I slept most of the time. By the second week, I began watching television and reading, activities that soon became monotonous. My thoughts ran rampant, and I longed to be active again. During the last three weeks of recuperation, I vowed not to complain about my life ever again. If work tired me, I would rest, but not complain. Managing responsibilities, however stressful, is more fun than being marooned on a couch. When we actually face the possibility of death, even the mundane in life becomes more treasured. Say yes to life now, while you can.

Say yes to love. Dickie and I are proud of our home. Neither one of us grew up in a house as large—though certainly not a mansion. We feel grateful that God has blessed us. The best way to say thanks to God was to share our house with others.

Our guest bedroom has been "home" to more than a dozen people through the years. Some lived with us only a week, others for a month or a year. One guest stayed three nights a week for five years. The sheer joy of getting to know these wonderful people raised our fun quotient to new levels.

Say yes to laughter. One morning a friend was driving me to the airport. We left in sufficient time to make the 9 a.m. departure; however, an accident had traffic at a standstill for miles. Nine o'clock came and went, and there we sat. Instead of becoming angry, we got out of the car and visited with other motorists, smiling and laughing along the way. Laughter didn't change the situation, but it did change us. We embraced the fun that was available at that moment and said, "Yes."

Think of a hundred more ways to say yes to life, love and laughter. To paraphrase Robert Frost's poem, "Stopping by Woods on a Snowy Evening," choose the road less traveled, and it will make all the difference.

87

Aim for the trash can.

Wad up some paper and aim for the trash can. Tossing trash creates a delightful diversion. You are simultaneously working and having fun. You are remaining light-hearted and playful while performing mundane tasks.

Make a game out of sorting the mail. If you throw a piece of junk mail toward the can and miss, you are honor bound to open the contents and read it. If your trash can is positioned in an easily accessible spot, friends can share the fun as they pass your office and take a shot. Like playing basketball as a kid, this simple idea rejuvenates the child within us.

How good is your aim? Mine is awful but that didn't stop me from joining the girl's basketball team in junior high. Because I was one of the tallest girls in the class, I played a forward on the first string.

Early in the season, we were in a tie game with only seconds left on the clock. In a clever play that surprised even me, I stole the ball from my opponent and went dribbling down the court! No one was between the goal and me. As I neared the backboard and prepared for the shot, I tripped over my feet and stumbled out of the court, crashing into the brick wall of the gymnasium. The fans went crazy. The game ended in a tie.

Although, I'll never be a star basketball player, I'm still optimistic. If my aim improves with practice, I might win a doll at the county fair.

If throwing paper in a trash can isn't the game that interests you, apply the theory to something that does. Twirl a pencil through your fingers, or toss peanuts in the air and catch them in your mouth. Pick up a dropped pen with your toes. Take ordinary, non-thinking tasks and turn them into small bites of fun. With enough small bites you can serve up a whole day of enjoyment.

88

Do the unexpected.

A routine, if not periodically examined, will become a rut. A rut becomes a grave with both ends open. Don't let your spirit die from routine boredom. Occasionally, resuscitate yourself by doing something unexpected—unexpected by you and others.

I'll never forget one occasion when I was chaperoning at a camp located in the beautiful Smoky Mountains at Ridgecrest, North Carolina. The students were participating in an event in which they sat in a tire's inner tube, floated down a creek and plummeted over a six-foot waterfall into a deep pool of freezing cold water!

The adults stood in amazement on the banks. I'm not sure what happened to me. I was just standing there when a youngster challenged me, "Hey, Mrs. Walters! When are you going to try it?" Before I knew it, I was climbing up the rocky path, taking off my bathing suit wrap, getting in line, and waiting my turn to take the plunge.

Talk about "doing the unexpected!" The last thing I had expected to do that day was to get into a freezing creek. However, the thrill of that primitive ride gave an emotional charge to my fun quotient that lasted the rest of the week.

Like cold water in the face, a departure from a routine can prevent you from sleepwalking through life. Don't get to the end of your days and look back, wishing you had been more adventurous. Carpe diem! Do the unexpected!

89

Sing cheerful songs.

Go ahead! Sing! Can't think of a happy tune? How about "Zip-A-Dee-Doo-Dah" by Allie Wrubel and Ray Gilbert? The word "zip-a-dee" is hard to say without smiling.

> *Zip-a-dee-doo-dah, zip-a-dee-ay*
> *My, oh, my, what a wonderful day!*
> *Plenty of sunshine heading my way.*
> *Zip-a-dee-doo-dah, zip-a-dee-ay.*
> *Mister Bluebird's on my shoulder*
> *It's the truth; it's actch'll*
> *Ev'rything is satisfactch'll.*
> *Zip-a-dee-doo-dah, zip-a-dee-ay*
> *Wonderful feeling; wonderful day!*

Feeling better yet? Try driving to work one morning singing "Up, Up and Away" by Jim Webb. You might not even notice the traffic or the length of a red light.

Would you like to ride in my beautiful balloon?
Would you like to glide in my beautiful balloon?
We can float among the stars together, you and I,
For we can fly! We can fly!
Up, up and away, my beautiful, my beautiful balloon.

In the 1980s, I directed a high school show choir. We performed a wide variety of music for all types of audiences. The effect the music had on the audience was easy to see. Slow love songs, though pretty, rendered the audience quiet and still. Cheerful, up-tempo songs produced smiling faces, tapping feet and often clapping hands.

Singing cheerful songs adds a lot of humor to your life. If you don't know any songs, write your own. Make the words positive and pave the way for humor.

90

Create a joy room!

Create a joy room. Any room will do. A little room in a shed out back will suffice. The idea is to claim some small area that can be your retreat. Place things in the room that you enjoy, things that make you smile.

Lighting has a powerful effect on our moods. Low light tends to be soothing, while bright light is energizing. Do you like candles, lamps, overhead lights, colored or psychedelic lights? Determine what you generally need to bring you joy and equip your joy room accordingly.

Use a tape or CD player to fill your room with music— joyful music with happy lyrics and delightful melodies. Visit good memories by playing your favorite movie on a television and VCR.

Include your hobbies in the joy room. Anything you enjoy will do. Surround yourself with reminders of good things and happy times.

I love to travel, and I love coming home to sleep in my own bed, pet my own dog and control my own thermostat! Upon entering the front door of my house after a long trip, a loving presence seems to say, "Welcome home!" Most travelers can relate to this feeling, but you don't have to return from a long trip to feel the need to escape into the security of your own kingdom. One bad report or hectic day at work or frazzling experience with children is all it takes to appreciate a special place of escape.

Occasionally, you may want to share your joy room with someone you love. At other times you'll want it to be your private retreat. With any luck, you will emerge from your joy room regrouped and smiling.

SECTION V

SPIRITUAL FUN

91

Practice random acts of kindness.

"As we have therefore opportunity, let us do good unto all men." (Galatians 6:10a, KJV) Random acts of kindness are delightful ways to apply the "do good" principle.

Because I like to walk, parking places located close to a building aren't particularly important to me. To drive past an empty space and allow the vehicle behind me to have it is quite a thrill. Occasionally, I see the driver's surprised look in my rear view mirror. You can't buy that joyful feeling in any store, regardless of how close you park to the front door.

Dickie and I invited friends over for dinner one Friday night. When Friday afternoon arrived, I realized I had forgotten one tiny, but important detail—the dessert. I raced to a near-by grocery store to purchase a lemon pie. As I reached for the familiar yellow box, I saw a coupon that read "$1.50 Off Lemon Pie" lying on top. I could hardly believe it. Someone had obviously clipped the coupon and placed it carefully on the top pie. I looked in both directions for my benefactor. No one was around. Without further thought, I scampered to the check out lines, humming as I went. I told the cashier and other customers about my exciting find. I sang all the way home. I imagine the prudent shopper smiled when she placed the $1.50 coupon on the pie; but if she had any idea about the results of her gesture, her smile would surely have become a laugh.

As simple as a smile, as tangible as a gift, as grandiose as a sacrifice, random acts of kindness are natural agents of joy. Good deeds are contagious! When you are kind to people, most of them want to be kind back to you.

92

Fire up your faith.
Take a risk!

On most mornings when you awaken, you can predict the events and outcomes of the day—knowing exactly how every activity will start and end. Sometimes, just for the fun of it, you need to start something not knowing how it will end. In other words, you need to take a risk—accept a new position, start a new project, attempt something bigger than you ever have before. If God inspires that risk, hang on to your hat. You're in for the most fun-filled, faith-developing ride of your life!

I once attended the Moody Adams Evangelistic Crusade for a full week. On the last night, each family in the audience was asked to help support that ministry by donating $25. I took out my checkbook and looked at the balance.

Ten more days were left in the month and I only had $25 in the bank.

Giving the money seemed the right thing to do, so I took the risk, wrote the check, and began to wonder how God was going to help me survive until the end of the month. The very next day my phone rang. The marketing manager at a local TV station was shooting a commercial and needed a female actress. "Can you please come right now?" he asked. I accepted and in little more than an hour, I came home with a $50 check in my hand! Talk about fun!

A few days earlier, I had applied for a disc jockey position at a local radio station. The manager informed me that no positions were available. Slightly discouraged, I postponed applying to any other radio stations. You guessed it! Before the week was out, the station manager called and said he needed a Sunday Morning DJ to spin Christian music and air pre-recorded programs. The salary was $25 a Sunday. I earned $25 every Sunday morning for the next eight years and loved my "air time."

Fun is difficult to find in routine. Risk something. Faith and fun swim together in unexplored waters. Dive in.

93

Join a joyful church.

Grow spiritually and have fun at the same time—join a joy-ful church. More than just a body of believers who meet to worship, a joyful church is a fellowship. The schedule of programs offers a variety of activities, which give families and friends opportunities to bond.

I grew up in a small town with a Baptist church directly across the street from my house. As soon as I was old enough to go by myself, I spent hundreds of hours at that church. In addition to the regular Sunday morning and evening activities, I sang in youth choirs, directed children choirs, participated in Girls Auxiliary groups and Young Women's Missionary Unions. On many occasions, I can remember my daddy saying, "Janie, why don't we just buy you a cot so you can move into the church?"

If a cot had been an option, I would have readily agreed

with the idea. I loved church and everything that took place there. My friends were members, and we looked forward to seeing each other at every event. The pastor was a faithful man of God. The congregation was devoted to him, and his sermons encouraged us. Church was then, and still is today, a major source of fun.

A joyful church has activities for all age groups. Don't wait to be invited . . . just go!

94

Gaze at the stars.

Some evening, when the weather is comfortable and the sky is clear, take a blanket to the backyard or beach, spread it on the ground, lie down, and feast your eyes on the night-time canvas. You don't need a telescope to enjoy stargazing. Even if you don't recognize the Dippers or the North Star, your imagination will still have a field day. Invent your own groupings and give them names. Choose a favorite star and make a wish on it.

One night, after a full day of walking and shopping in the French Quarter of New Orleans, my friends and I stopped at the Café Du Monde to enjoy world-famous beignets and coffee. On this particular night, an astronomy student sat perched outside the café with a large telescope. For $1, a customer could gaze at the heavens. I slipped the student my dollar, looked into the eyepiece, and gasped.

There in the sky, already focused, was the planet Saturn. The famous three rings were clearly distinguishable. I had only seen the planet's rings in books, so I marveled at their reality. The young astronomer pointed out the Big Dipper and the Little Dipper, making sure I saw Polaris, better known as the North Star. We all took a turn gazing into the night sky.

When you gaze at the stars, find the brightest star and recall the special star seen by shepherds over 2,000 years ago. Try to re-create the joy the shepherds felt when the angels appeared unto them and said, "Fear not, for, behold, I bring you good tidings of great joy, which shall be to all people. For unto you is born this day in the city of David, a Savior, which is Christ the Lord." (Luke 2:10-11, KJV) To maximize the fun, personalize that scripture and believe it.

95

Go on a mission trip.

Opportunities for mission trips abound in churches, the Peace Corps, the American Red Cross and other organizations. These opportunities give you a chance to make a difference in the world. Just knowing that your life has made a difference is a tremendous source of fun.

Years ago, I answered the call to San Juan, Puerto Rico, where a small church was building a Christian junior high school. Other church groups had constructed the large, two-story frame building. Our job was to paint. From sunup to sundown for a week, we climbed on scaffolding, hung from banisters, and squatted on floors, slapping paint on all wooden surfaces.

At the end of each day, we drove to the ocean and jumped into the cool water fully dressed in our sweat-drenched clothing. After dinner, we shared stories about the day. We studied the Bible, prayed, and laughed a lot.

We didn't fully realize the difference 13 people could make until the day we left. We stood in what would eventually be the playground and looked at the building. We had been in the building, on the building, and under the building, but we had never stepped back to look *at* the building. Much to our amazement, the junior high school was beautiful.

Before we headed back to the airport, the pastor of the small church and a few of his faithful members walked over to say goodbye. Though words were said, none were needed. We knew our work was appreciated and we had made a difference in the lives of an entire community.

A "mission trip" doesn't have to be to another country or state. A "mission" can be just across the street if we go with the purpose of helping someone. The concept is a super stress reliever because it takes our minds off of ourselves. Take a few friends with you and multiply the fun. This assignment is a mission that is possible. Don't miss out on your trip!

96

Praise God!

To remain in a happy, confident state, acknowledge the greatness of God, enumerate His qualities, and remind yourself of the power He has to heal you, bless you, fight for you, empower you, protect you, forgive you, and make you new.

The salesman on the telephone seemed to have all the right answers. I asked as many questions as I knew to ask, and even said, "I understand," when he mentioned that the fee of $3,000 for a year's service was non-refundable. I eagerly recited to him my credit card number. When I told Dickie about the purchase, he asked questions about the service for which I had no answers. He sensed it was an unwise purchase and asked me to cancel the order. When I called, I was reminded that the program was non-refundable. I had a major problem. Dickie wanted me out of the program, and "they" wanted me in. I cried a lot that week.

When Sunday morning arrived, I applied waterproof make-up to my swollen eyes and went to the early praise and worship service. The words of the first song were based in scripture: "Enter into His gates with thanksgiving and into His courts with praise." (Psalms 100:4, KJV) The song declared, "I will rejoice for He has made me glad." (Psalms 21:6, KJV) I thought, "If anybody can make me glad, God can. No problem is too great for Him. The whole universe belongs to Him. He owns the cattle on a thousand hills, $3,000 is nothing to Him."

As I continued to sing, my faith began to rise. For the first time in days, a spark of joy flickered. I believed that whatever happened, Dickie and I would be all right. By the time the service ended, my spirit shouted, "All things work together for good to them that love the Lord, and are called according to His purpose." (Romans 8:28, KJV)

As for the $3,000, I didn't have to pay it. The company eventually agreed to a misunderstanding by both parties. I learned a valuable lesson about telephone solicitation, but the best lesson I learned was about the power of praise to restore fun to my life. Praise really works.

97

Bury the hatchet.

"Fore" means "to come first, in front of." For(e)giveness implies an attitude that is extended to a person prior to the hurt. If sorrow and anger come after disappointments, the wise choice is to decide in advance to forgive others so that your joy can remain intact. After all, Jesus said from the cross, "Father, forgive them for they know not what they do." (Luke 23:34, KJV)

Housekeeping is a subject that has generated many arguments in my marriage. I tend to clutter an area, leaving shoes in the living room and books on the dining table. Dickie insists that everything should have a specific place and be in it . . . all the time.

One afternoon I found my bedroom dresser piled high with "stuff." Purses, cups, blouses and more were stacked on it. "What have you done?" I exclaimed. "I just straightened up the house," was his innocent reply. I went from exasperated to furious. "If you were going to take the time to gather all of these items, why didn't you put them where they belonged?"

That question launched a heated discussion. Finally, I agreed to keep all rooms that were frequented by guests uncluttered, and Dickie agreed that my side of the bedroom was my personality's haven. Even though I agreed to the compromise, I inwardly stewed about it. Then one day, forgiveness walked in the door. Actually, they were guests who stopped by for an unexpected visit. Instead of shoving things into closets and under couches, I joyfully invited them in and toured them through our home. Thanks to Dickie, the house was clean. Appreciation replaced frustration.

If you forgive the person for a hurt, you open your heart to healing. Making up with the offending party can be fun, especially if that party is your spouse. And when you forgive, bury the hatchet and don't mark the spot.

98

Count your blessings.

Reflect upon the blessings in your life and make a thanksgiving list. Your list can include your family that loves you, friends to share good times with, finally landing that dream job, the clothes on your back . . . you name it. Let your list become a game. Can you think of 100 blessings in the next 10 minutes? That's 10 blessings a minute!

In 1980, I was a young teacher, engaged to Dickie, without a care in the world. The two of us were at a friend's house when a terrible rainstorm began. We turned on the news and learned that, after being struck by lightning, the apartment complex where I lived was on fire. We quickly drove toward the complex but were stopped by police barricades. We left the car and walked as close as we could.

Tenants huddled on the lawn, watching the fire leap in and out of windows. Occasionally, someone wailed, "Everything I own is gone. What am I going to do?" Dickie told me it would be okay if I wanted to cry. "Why should I cry," I thought. "The apartment was filled with *things*. All of them can be replaced." I was just thankful no one was hurt.

Then in 1999, I was visiting a friend in Florida when I received a phone call from Dickie telling me that our house had been struck by lightning. Once I realized he was OK and the contents of the house were basically safe, I didn't think much more about the house that night.

Based on my earlier experience, I was surprised when the next afternoon I started to feel depressed. Luckily, wisdom and reasoning took over, prompted surely by the Holy Spirit. I sat down and made my thanksgiving list. Mostly, I thanked God that Dickie and I had income that would allow us to pay for the repairs. In addition, I was grateful for all the things that didn't happen. The house didn't burn down, I didn't lose all my photographs and books, and we weren't vacationing in Paris when it happened. By the time I finished the thanksgiving list, my joy was restored. I felt lucky!

The race is on. Start your list NOW!

99

Memorize scripture.

If you keep something with you all the time, you rarely have to look for it. That's why memorizing Bible scriptures is such a great idea. You can carry them with you always, and the scriptures' wisdom and encouragement will be there for you when you need them. To make the memorization process fun, invite your friends to join you and make a game of it. Scriptures can be life changing.

Mrs. Thompson was a proper, reserved pastor's wife, faithful in her duties to the church. One of her projects was preparing 8- to 12-year-olds for the annual statewide "Sword Drill Contest." "Sword" referred to the Bible, and we had to learn to "draw it and use it."

For five years, my church friends and I went to Mrs. Thompson's house every Saturday morning and practically memorized the Bible. We learned to recite the names of all

66 books, in order. Decades later, I can still recite all of them. In addition, we memorized hundreds of scriptures and were trained to locate them in 10 seconds or less.

One of my fond memories of my mother took place while I was preparing for the sword drill. We were sitting on our front porch one Saturday morning at 8 o'clock. Mom was still wearing her white nurse's uniform and I was still in pajamas. She had just come home from the midnight shift at the hospital and had pulled me out of bed to drill me on the scriptures. Half asleep, I complained, "Why are you doing this to me?" She replied, "Because Mrs. Thompson will skin both of us if you don't learn these scriptures!" Our laughter woke me up, and I managed to pass that Saturday's inspection.

Let me challenge you to devise your own "sword drill." Get together with friends and make a game of it. Though you have the whole Bible to choose from, why not start with the following:

"For God so loved the world that He gave His only begotten Son, that whosoever believeth in Him, shall not perish but have eternal life. (John 3:16, KJV)

100

Look for miracles.

Many miracles are supernatural and leave the logic of man spinning. Stories abound of blind men receiving sight, incurable cancers being healed, and survivors climbing out of wrecked cars unscathed in what should have been fatal crashes. Great excitement accompanies these miracles! In order to experience some of that excitement on a regular basis, keep your eyes open for the dozens of little miracles that happen every day.

I was in the sixth grade when I first understood that miracles happen every day. That year for Christmas, my parents had given me a nice watch, and I was proud of its delicate design and small gold band with a tiny security chain. You can imagine my horror when I looked down during history class and noticed the crystal on the face of the watch was missing. My friends and I, just minutes before, had been playing basketball during recess. Surely the missing crystal was out there somewhere. I begged the teacher for permission to go back to the playground. The teacher said something about a needle in a haystack and sent me on my way.

As I ran to the playground, I prayed for God to help me in my search. The playground had a clay and dirt surface, and dust could easily cover the small crystal and hide it from view. Nevertheless, I began to walk in a large square pattern around the basketball area, much like I had seen Dad do when he was mowing the front lawn. Within minutes, my eyes fell on a glittering object reflecting the sun's rays. That object was my crystal—dusty, but not scratched!

Elated, I ran back to class. When he heard the news, my teacher exclaimed, "Janie, that's a miracle!" I knew he was right. God had given me a little miracle that day. The experience created so much joy that my child-like faith grew to expect other miracles.

Miracles are thrilling, and we praise God for them. However, if we fail to spot the little miracles that happen every day, we are missing a huge source of fun.

101

Rejoice in all things.

When joy starts to wane, magnify that joyful feeling through re-use. The process goes like this: you have joy, then you "re-joy," and keep "re-joicing" until the spiritual victory is yours. The fun is not only in the challenge, but also in the result.

Chuck Colson's name was recognized by millions of Americans. He had risen from a simple lawyer to become an advisor to the President of the United States. Caught in the Watergate Scandal during Richard Nixon's administration, Chuck became a fall guy for the incident and swapped his celebrity status for a cell. Yet, he testifies that prison was one of the best things that ever happened to him.

So how could this experience be the best thing that ever

happened to Colson? He accepted Jesus as his Savior and Lord in prison. That one new friend changed Colson's life for eternity and gave him a ministry to prisoners.

I certainly don't believe God causes bad things to happen to us, but I know He allows them to occur. In Matthew 5:45 (KJV), Jesus taught, ". . . God maketh His sun to rise on the evil and on the good, and sendeth rain on the just and the unjust."

For those times when you rejoice one minute and are tormented by despair the next, recycle your joy. First, claim your joy, which simply means to make a decision to be joyful regardless of what your circumstances are. Then, start telling people about your joy, broadcasting the good news of your decision. Finally, keep rejoicing—talking about it, singing about it, acting like you are happy—until your heart is overflowing with delight, totally dispelling despair. You can have perfect confidence that "All things will work together for your good if you love the Lord and are called according to His purposes." (Romans 8:28, KJV)

Acknowledgments

A published book is never the product of just one person's work. The combined efforts of many people are required. In the case of *Blow a Bubble Not a Gasket,* any attempt to name everyone who helped with this project is doomed to failure. So, let me at the outset say a huge THANK YOU to everyone who has ever done or said anything to encourage me in the writing of this book. I truly appreciate your help, and I ask for God's blessings upon your lives. More specifically, I wish to thank several people who have provided critical help along the way.

To Barney and Gwen McKee, the owners and publishers of Quail Ridge Press: thank you for meeting with me and listening to the thousands of words I produced in presenting my book's proposal. Thank you for believing in, and taking a risk on, an unknown writer. I will forever be in your debt.

To Keena Grissom, the editor assigned to the incredible task of unifying the form and language of a book that was written during a period of more than eight years: thank you for your vision, for your expertise at editing, for your work in assembling the pages, and for your relentless enthusiasm for the project. *Blow a Bubble Not a Gasket* is a better book because of your hand in it.

To Sheila Williams, the Associate Publisher at Quail Ridge Press who took the time to travel more than 200 miles to hear me speak and returned to convince her colleagues that the book would sell: thank you for your enthusiasm, for embracing the potential of a new author, and for your work in assembling the book.

To Cyndi Clark, Art Director: thank you for your layout and design of the book's cover and pages. I'm very proud of the way *Blow a Bubble Not a Gasket* looks, and the basic concept was all yours.

To Jimmie Saucier, Director of Sales and Marketing: thank you for believing in "Bubbles," for encouraging me, and for all of your efforts in getting the book off of the presses and into the hands of readers.

To all the staff at Quail Ridge Press: thank you for being true professionals and for embracing *Blow a Bubble Not a Gasket* with enthusiasm, expertise, and excellence.

To all the people who have periodically read my manuscript through the years and offered suggestions for edits (you know who you are—fellow English teachers, friends, and family): thank you for helping me "say what I meant, and say it in the right way." Specifically, thank you to Opal Worthy who not only edited my work at times, but also provided me with gems of wisdom that encouraged me through the process.

To Barry and Ann Morris: thank you for challenging me with a deadline and holding me accountable for it. *Blow a Bubble Not a Gasket* might still be on the drawing board without you.

To Billy Dugger, owner of The Mail Room Photo Lab: thank you for being the best photographer a girl could ever hope to have as a friend.

To Carol Szymanski, artist and graphic illustrator: thank you for the creative proposal sketches that helped me prepare for my initial meeting with my publishers.

To Jennifer West Signs, attorney: thank you for helping me work out contract details and always being handy with legal advice in which I can have confidence.

To Wanda Saul: thank you for blowing bubbles with me in my backyard. In addition to being a great memory, that experience gave birth to the title of this book.

To my husband Dickie, and my brother, sister-in-law, and niece—J. Brantly, Sandra, and Heather Still—and all of my other family members and friends who have allowed our shared stories to be recorded in *Blow a Bubble Not a Gasket:* thank you for being a part of my life and giving me so much material from which to draw.

To my beloved parents, William Thomas and Edna Cooper Still (both now in Heaven): thank you for providing the kind of family life where a child's sense of humor could develop and thrive. Thank you, also, for providing a loving, forgiving Christian foundation that gave me the confidence to take risks and taught me to put my faith and trust in God.

Finally, a special "thank you" is given to God, the author and sustainer of all mankind. Thank you for loving me and saving me and calling me to serve you. Thank you for sending all of these people to help me with this project. *I truly appreciate You.*

Bibliography

Bacon, Sir Francis. *Bartlett's Familiar Quotations* 15th ed. Bartlett, John, compiler. Boston: Little, Brown and Company, 1980.

Brown, Lew; Henderson, Ray; Rose, Billy. "The Dummy Song." New York: Shapiro, Bernstein & Co., Inc. and Ray Henderson Music Company, 1944. Recorded by Louis Armstrong.

Colson, Charles W. *Born Again.* Old Tappan, N.J.: Chosen Books, 1976.

Cook, Robert A. *Quotable Quotations.* Cory, Lloyd; compiler. Wheaton, Ill.: Victor Books, 1985.

Cousins, Norman. *The Anatomy of an Illness as Perceived by the Patient.* New York: Norton, 1979.

Davenport, Rita. *Laugh Your Way to Success: Success Skills with a Sense of Humor.* Phoenix, Ariz.: Davenport, 1991.

Fitzgerald, F. Scott. 1896-1940; Wilson, Edmund. *The Crack-up.* New York: J. Laughlin, 1945.

Foreman, Ed. *How to Make Every Day a Terrific Day.* Dallas, Texas: Executive Development Systems, 1991.

Frost, Robert. "Stopping by Woods on a Snowy Evening." *American Poetry and Prose.* Boston: Houghton Mifflin, 1970.

Holy Bible: containing the Old and New Testaments, authorized King James version, red letter edition. Nashville: Thomas Nelson, 1975.

Kipling, Rudyard. "If." *The Best Loved Poems of the American People.* New York: Doubleday & Company, 1936.

Leigh, Mitch; Wasserman, Dale; Darion, Joseph. *Man of La Mancha; A Musical Play.* New York: Random House, 1966.

McNally, Terrance. *Lips Together, Teeth Apart.* New York: Dramatists Play Service, 1992.

Merriam-Webster's Collegiate Dictionary 10th ed. Springfield, Mass.: Merriam-Webster, 1993.

Nash, Ogden. "A Jolly Young Fellow From Yuma." *The Penguin Book of Limericks.* E. O. Parrott, ed. New York: Penguin Books, 1983.

Peale, Norman Vincent. *The Power of Positive Thinking.* New York: Prentice-Hall, 1952.

Piper, Watty. *The Little Engine That Could.* New York: Platt & Munk, 1976.

Sherman, Richard M.; Sherman, Robert B. "A Spoonful of Sugar" from *Walt Disney's Mary Poppins.* Milwaukee, Wis.: Wonderland Music Co.; Hal Leonard distributor, 2002.

Smyth, Bambi. "This Little Piggy Went to Market." Noble Park, Australia: Five Mile Press, 1995.

Steinbeck, John. *Quotable Quotations.* Cory, Lloyd; Compiler. Wheaton, Ill.: Victor Books, 1985.

Thoreau, Henry David. *A Week on the Concord and Merrimack Rivers; Walden, or Life in the Woods; the Maine Woods; Cape Cod.* New York: Viking Press, 1985.

Webb, Jimmy; Hayward, Lou. "Up, Up and Away" Delaware Water Gap, Penn.: Shawnee, 1969. Recorded by 5th Dimension.

Wrubel, Allie; Gilbert, Ray; Forsblad, Leland. "Zip-a-dee-doo-dah" from *Walt Disney's Song of the South.* Winona, Minn.: Hal Leonard Publishing, 1975.

Ziglar, Zig. *See You at the Top.* Gretna, Louisiana: Pelican Publishing Co., 1979.

Champion Communications

The following keynotes and/or workshops, conducted by Janie Walters, are designed to equip people with the communication skills needed to seize the best life has to offer and to encourage them to offer their best back to life.

For more information or to schedule an appearance, contact:
Janie Walters, Champion Communications
Phone / Fax: 601-607-2979 • Email: joyfullyjanie@aol.com
www.janiewalters.com

Workshops available:

- **BLOW A BUBBLE NOT A GASKET**
  Stress Management Techniques that Work
- **POPEYE AND POPSICLES** or **POP GOES THE WEASEL!**
  The Importance of Humor in the Workplace
- **THE GARBAGE TRUCK COMES ON TUESDAYS AND FRIDAYS**
  Neutralizing Negatives
- **NORMAL IS GONE AND IT WON'T BE BACK**
  Coping with and Embracing Change
- **YOU SAID WHAT?!?#$%^$!??**
  Communicating Effectively: Listening and Speaking, In that Order
- **IT'S BEEN A PLEASURE DOING BUSINESS WITH YOU**
  Customer Service Redefined / Salesmanship Skills
- **WHEN YOUR BLOOD STARTS BOILING, DON'T LET IT COOK
  YOUR GOOSE** Conflict Resolution and Anger Management
- **A NEW DAY OR JUST ANOTHER ONE?**
  Shaping Tomorrow with the Plans Made Today
- **EFFECTIVE PUBLIC SPEAKING: EVEN IF YOUR KNEES ARE
  KNOCKING**
- **TEAMWORK: UNITED WE STAND, DIVIDED WE NEED EXCEDRIN**
- **TO BOLDLY GO WHERE NO MAN HAS EVER GONE BEFORE**
  Leadership in the Year 2000 and Beyond
- **KUDZU OR KUDOS?** The Motivating Power of Praise
- **THREE CHEERS FOR US!**
  Building Self-Esteem in Ourselves and Others

ORDER FORM

Motivational Cassettes, CDs, and Books

To order, send check, money order or credit card information to:
Champion Communications • P. O. Box 443 • Madison, MS 39130-0443
Phone / Fax: 601-607-2979 • Email: joyfullyjanie@aol.com
Order online at: www.janiewalters.com

Name _____   Phone # _____

Address _____

City/State/Zip _____

Email Address _____

❏ Check or money order enclosed   Charge to: ❏ Visa ❏ MasterCard

Card # _____   Expiration Date _____

Signature _____

Qty.	Title	Cassette	CD	Total
	Humor for Life	$6.00	$8.00	
	The Garbage Truck Comes on Tuesdays and Fridays	$6.00	$8.00	
	Three Cheers for Us: Developing Self Esteem	$6.00	$8.00	
	Normal Is Gone and It Won't Be Back	$6.00	$8.00	
	Develop the Habit of Joy: 21-Day Devotional (Book $5.00)			
	Blow a Bubble Not a Gasket (Book $8.95)			

Subtotal _____

Postage rates:
- $1.50 for orders under $20.00.
- $3.00 for orders totalling
  $20.00 or more.

7% Tax for MS residents _____

Postage (see chart) _____

Total enclosed _____